Expand Your English

Expand Your English

A Guide to Improving Your Academic Vocabulary

Steve Hart

HKU
PRESS
香港大學出版社

Hong Kong University Press
The University of Hong Kong
Pokfulam Road
Hong Kong
www.hkupress.hku.hk

ISBN 978-988-8390-99-1 (*Paperback*)

British Library Cataloguing-in-Publication Data
A catalogue record for this book is available from the British Library.

10 9 8 7 6 5 4 3 2

Printed and bound by Paramount Printing Co., Ltd., Hong Kong, China

CONTENTS

Introduction

A strong ambition of many non-native English writers is to expand their vocabulary. One of the best ways to approach this is by reading as much as possible. Many learners also use dictionaries and word lists to try to increase the number of words they know. But how effective are these resources, and how many words are actually retained and, importantly, employed by writers in their essays and assignments?

The answer is likely to be very few. While reading and looking up words in a dictionary can improve receptive vocabulary (understanding words when hearing or reading them), it is less effective for developing productive vocabulary (actively producing appropriate words when writing). Learners often feel frustrated when writing in English because they cannot find the words to express their ideas effectively. The reason is primarily the limited words at their disposal and the worry that the words they do know are too 'unacademic' and therefore unsuitable. Increasing one's receptive vocabulary is certainly useful, but productive vocabulary is the key to writing well in English and producing good academic work. *Expand Your English* has been designed for this purpose, by targeting 200 key academic phrases* that learners may well have heard of, or even know how to use, but probably do not use as often as they should in their writing. Some of the terms may seem fairly obvious or familiar, but often non-native speakers fail to employ them in their writing and either fall back on the 'safe' elementary term or use a phrase or metaphor picked up socially. It is also important to remember

---

* The 200 terms were chosen based on how frequently they occur in academic writing (drawn from three academic corpora), how useful they are to non-native speakers, and how likely they are to be missing from a learner's productive vocabulary. They were selected after consulting three academic written English corpora: the British Academic Written English Corpus (BAWE), the academic word list of the Corpus of Contemporary American English (COCA), and the academic word list devised by Averil Coxhead at the University of Wellington. COCA listed the words by the frequency with which they occurred in published academic texts, so this was used as a base upon which I added the other two word lists and looked for matches. Words featuring in West's General Service List (GSL) (1953) were rejected, as were any others deemed by me to be in frequent current use (after consulting my own personal collection of 600 essays written by Chinese postgraduates—on the condition they had been used correctly—that I had proofread between 2006 and 2015). The terms appearing only on a subject-specific list were then further scrutinized for their suitability. The most frequent 200 words (top of the COCA frequency list plus featuring in BAWE and Coxhead minus appearing in West and rejected through my own judgement) were then selected, and an attempt was made to include the remaining 1,000 or so in Part B of the book.

that there is just as much worth in knowing when not to use a certain word as when to use it.

There are three key areas to consider when trying to increase productive vocabulary, and these are the foundation of *Expand Your English*. They are essential to retaining the learnt words and retrieving them when needed.

Understanding: knowing the various definitions of the term and the words the term is used alongside

Context: knowing when and how to use the term

Familiarity: encountering the term regularly and in various contexts

In order for writers to retain, retrieve, and reuse the 200 terms that form Part A of the book, they have been divided up into sets of ten. Each set is introduced and then revisited. The three areas (understanding, context, and familiarity) that the book concentrates on will aid this process of remembering and retaining.

In this part, the reader may choose to tackle each set of ten terms in order and work his or her way through the book. Alternatively, an effective way to retain and embed the terms into memory is to read the first stage of each set, do the first checks, and then move on to set two. Once all twenty sets have been read and the questions answered, the reader can advance to the second stage of set one and so on.

BEGIN
SET 1 First stage: read through
SET 1 First check: complete the exercises
SET 2 First stage: read through
SET 2 First check: complete the exercises

When all the first stages are complete, proceed to the second stages.

SET 1 Second stage: read through
SET 1 Second check: complete the exercises

The second part of the book categorizes key academic terms according to function, meaning, and the areas of an essay in which they are likely to be relevant. Again, context and familiarity are the objectives. Some of the 200 key words reappear in this part, to reinforce the learning. An index is also provided, with chapter numbers rather than page numbers to encourage the reader to search for the term within the entries and form links rather than be directed to the exact location.

Dictionaries are usually consulted only when a new word is encountered. *Expand Your English* shows the learner which words to encounter for effective and professional academic writing. As mentioned, the only way to increase productive vocabulary is to explore words in detail and to keep revisiting them—that is the reason part one is dedicated to only a handful of words. Revisiting the terms later (having learnt many others in between) will help the reader to embed the terms and increase their familiarity. Soon they will be in productive vocabulary ready for the next assignment.

It is a pity when good subject knowledge and creative ideas are undermined by weak or repetitive writing. The 200 key terms and countless others contained in *Expand Your English* will go a long way to preventing this common problem from occurring in the papers of students and researchers at academic institutions.

Acknowledgements

The author wishes to thank Susie Han of Hong Kong University Press for her enthusiasm, diligence, valued comments, and swift correspondence.

Steve Hart
2016

Part A

Two Hundred
Key Academic Terms

The definitions, collocations, and contexts of use for 200 academic terms are provided in this section. Usage notes give further explanation where needed, and exercises after each section test the understanding of both meaning and suitability.

Part A

Two Hundred
Key Academic Terms

1

accomplish accumulate acquire actively adhere adjustment advanced advent advocate align

First stage: Introducing the terms

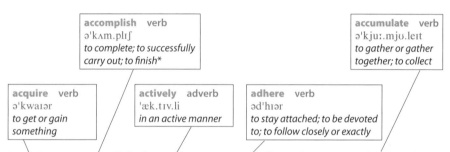

accomplish verb
ə'kʌm.plɪʃ
to complete; to successfully carry out; to finish*

accumulate verb
ə'kjuː.mjʊ.leɪt
to gather or gather together; to collect

acquire verb
ə'kwaɪər
to get or gain something

actively adverb
'æk.tɪv.li
in an active manner

adhere verb
əd'hɪər
to stay attached; to be devoted to; to follow closely or exactly

In order to **accomplish** these objectives, we will need to **accumulate** evidence over the course of the three observation sessions. Once the evidence has been **acquired**, we can **actively** seek participants for phase two. As with the initial phase, phase two will **adhere** to the university's policy on ethics (see Appendix 3).

Any **advanced** study will require the researcher to make **adjustments** at some stage. Most guidelines also **advocate** the use of backup files. With the **advent** of 'smart' software, we have been able to **align** multiple aspects of the study and plan effectively.

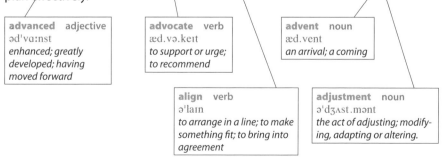

advanced adjective
əd'vɑːnst
enhanced; greatly developed; having moved forward

advocate verb
æd.və.keɪt
to support or urge; to recommend

advent noun
æd.vent
an arrival; a coming

align verb
ə'laɪn
to arrange in a line; to make something fit; to bring into agreement

adjustment noun
ə'dʒʌst.mənt
the act of adjusting; modifying, adapting or altering.

---

* The definitions used throughout this book have been obtained from Cambridge Learners online dictionary, dictionary.com, the free dictionary online, Merriam Webster's online dictionary, or a combination of them.

📋 First check

A   Circle the verbs in this list.

adjustment   accumulate   acquire   advent   adhere   align

B   Select a word from the ten key terms to match each definition.

in an active manner   _____

to successfully carry out   _____

an arrival   _____

to bring into relation or agreement   _____

C   Underline the terms that are misspelled in this extract.

This information can be aquired fairly easily, but ajustments will need to be made to reporting to aline with other companies in the industry. This will be actively pursued in April, so the firm can accomplish the aims set out in Document 12. Hopefully, this will lead to acculminating more revenue.

Second stage: Collocations and usage

Accomplish   is a regular verb. Its past participle is accomplished and its present participle is accomplishing. It has a related noun form, accomplishment.

> **Better than** do, get done *What does this mean?* Well, instead of writing 'do' or 'get done', you could choose the more academic term 'accomplish'.

Accomplish is often used alongside the nouns 'aim', 'goal', 'objective', and 'task'.

It will also indicate how to accomplish the aims set out in section three.

Explaining the task was the next step. This was accomplished by asking the three demonstrators to . . .

Usage notes: 'Accomplish' is usually employed in its past participle form to explain how something was done. 'Achieve' is also an option.

The aim was to provide a representative sample. This was accomplished/ achieved through the use of . . .

When describing a person, the past participle has a different meaning. Here it suggests 'highly trained or skilled'.

He was an accomplished scholar and developed several theories relating to . . .

Accumulate is a regular verb. Its past participle is accumulated and its present participle is accumulating. It has a related noun form, accumulation.

Better than add, amass

Accumulate is often used alongside 'evidence' and 'knowledge'.

The next step was to accumulate all the evidence.*

Knowledge of the system will need to be accumulated at some stage.

It is commonly used with the adverbs 'gradually' and 'rapidly'.

These errors accumulate rapidly if unchecked.

Usage notes: There are two points to consider here. First, the spelling: it is 'accumulate' not 'acculminate'. Second, there is no need to follow the verb with 'together'. *All the evidence was then accumulated together.*

Acquire is a regular verb. Its past participle is acquired and its present participle is acquiring. It has a related noun form, acquisition.

Better than get, get hold of

It is often employed alongside the nouns 'information', 'knowledge', and 'skills'.

This information can be acquired from a number of sources.

Learners will acquire knowledge almost immediately.

Unfortunately, she did not acquire any language skills during the course.

---

* The examples used throughout the book are from the essays of Chinese postgraduate students. Each one has been carefully modified to ensure anonymity while retaining the essence of the sentence.

Actively   is an adverb that usually comes before the verb it is modifying.

Better than keenly, energetically, really

Actively is used with a variety of verbs, including 'encourage', 'engage', 'involve', 'participate', 'promote', 'seek', and 'support'.

We need to actively encourage this behaviour in order for it to spread throughout the organization.

Usage notes: As with most adverbs, the writer needs to ask whether the verb actually requires an adverb, as it might be strong enough on its own. 'Actively' is useful when emphasizing that a real effort is being made. *They are actively working to change perceptions of this often-persecuted group.*

Adhere   is a regular verb. Its past participle is adhered and its present participle is adhering. It has related noun forms, adherence and adherent.

Better than obey, stick to, follow

Adhere is used with a variety of nouns, the most common being 'guidelines', 'principles', 'procedures', 'rules', 'standards', and 'traditions'. The preposition 'to' always follows adhere.

The procedures are bound to provide successful results once they are adhered to effectively.

I will adhere to these ethical guidelines throughout the process.

Usage notes: The noun form 'adherent' names a person who is a supporter or believer of a group, party, theory, or set of ideas. (See also 21.)

She is an adherent of the Belton Method.

Adjustment   is a countable noun with a related verb form, adjust.

Better than change, tweak

This also allows behavioural adjustments to be made, as an entrepreneur may have different options available.

Usage notes: Adjustment works well when discussing small changes, as in 'minor adjustment' or 'slight adjustment'. Often, adjustment is used for when something physically needs to be moved; when reports or models need to be changed, then 'alteration' or 'amendment' is better.

Advanced   is an adjective that can be used directly before a noun to modify it (e.g., *an advanced case*) or after a linking verb* (e.g., *It seemed advanced*). It is the past participle of the verb advance. The related noun form is advancement.

Better than later, better, complicated, ahead

Advanced is used with a variety of nouns including 'case', 'degree', 'level', 'skills', 'system', 'technology', and 'technique'. Here are examples of the two ways to use the adjective—the first as a noun modifier and the second with a verb.

It is an advanced system and therefore requires little manual input.

We require a system that is not only advanced but also user-friendly.

Usage notes: Advanced has several meanings. The most common relate to something being progressive or innovative and something that is complex or at a higher level. Unlike most past participles, advanced can be used in an active way when modifying the noun (instead of just having a passive meaning).

Advent   is a noun and is often used as part of a phrase. There are five common expressions that 'advent' occurs in, all of which end in 'of'.

Better than beginning, start

Before the _____ of   Following the _____ of

Since the _____ of   Until the _____ of   With the _____ of

It can also be used between a definite article and 'of'.

The advent of heterogeneous architectures in mainstream industry had a significant influence on mainstream software.

Advocate   is a regular verb. Its past participle is advocated and its present participle is advocating. It has related noun forms, advocate and advocacy.

Better than back, follow, stand up for

Spera (2005) advocated that it is critical for families and schools to work together.

---

* Linking verbs connect the subject of the sentence to words (e.g., adjectives) that are describing the subject. The key linking verb is *to be* (with its various forms *am, is, are, was, were*). Other linking verbs include *appear, become, feel, grow, look, prove, remain, seem, smell, sound, taste, turn*.

Usage notes: Advocate is usually employed when an expert or someone with experience gives support or backs something.

The Ministry advocates the use of this system in schools.

The noun form 'advocate' is spelled the same as the verb but pronounced differently. Verb, 'æd.və.keɪt, noun, 'æd.və.kət (note the extended ending on the verb). The noun refers to someone who supports something (see also 21).

He is an advocate of student-centered learning.

Align is a regular verb. Its past participle is aligned and its present participle is aligning. It has related noun forms, alignment and realignment.

Better than make straight, line up, side with

Align can be used with or without an object. When an object is used, the verb is often followed by 'with'.

Obviously, the two paths at some stage need to align.

The measures taken will need to align with the mission statement.

It is often used with the following plural nouns: 'efforts', 'interests', 'policies', 'programmes'.

When their interests align, we see a more productive environment.

Certain adverbs can be used with align including 'closely', 'naturally', and 'perfectly'.

Their methods needed to be closely aligned with institutional policy.

Usage notes: Align has two distinct meanings. The first is to line two things up so they are straight, either in a physical, literal sense or by concepts or ideas. The second is to show that someone or something supports or is in agreement with something else; for instance, the views of two people could align.

Again, an assessment should be made on whether the emphasis of the adverb is really adding anything to the verb. Saying that something aligns is sufficient most of the time (without the need for 'closely' or 'exactly'), because the verb alone implies that the two things are parallel or a match.

📋 Second check

A Which of the ten key terms do these synonyms relate to? The first one has been done for you.

change, alteration ** adjustment **

encourage, support   _____

obtain, secure   _____

observe, follow   _____

B Replace the struck-through word with a word from the ten available.

With the ~~start~~ _____ of the Jazz Age came a new outlook on how to ...

A simple ~~change~~ _____ to the speed should resolve the issue.

This will only occur once the *most* ~~complex~~ _____ method has been employed by the participants.

We ~~got~~ _____ this beaker from Cao Pharmaceuticals, Shenzhen.

C Select an appropriate option to match the key term.

This will easily align to/from/with the goals of the company.

Would they adhere with/to/on these measures if asked?

It will slightly/gradually/tentatively accumulate over time.

2

allege alleviate allocate ambiguity amendment apparatus apparent applicable arbitrary arguably

First stage: Introducing the terms

allege verb
əˈledʒ
to say or assert something without proof

arguably adverb
ˈɑːg.ju.ə.bli
that can be shown to be true; that can be argued

ambiguity noun
ˌæm.bɪˈgjuː.ə.ti
uncertainty of meaning; interpreting something in more than one way

amendment noun
əˈmend.mənt
an alteration; a correction

allocate verb
ˈæl.ə.keɪt
to assign something for a particular purpose; to distribute

The authors **allege** that senior managers must **allocate** time for staff to ask questions. An **amendment** to the working day such as this will, **arguably**, lead to less **ambiguity** in the weekly reports and **alleviate** the burden on the staff that have to make cross-disciplinary decisions. The **apparatus** currently in place to report queries is **arbitrary** and unstructured, and it is increasingly **apparent** that these current measures are only **applicable** to staff with full-time line managers.

arbitrary adj
ˈɑː.bɪ.trər.i
unsupported; based on chance; having only relative relevance

alleviate verb
əˈliː.vi.eɪt
to make something easier to bear; to lessen or relieve

apparatus noun
æp.əˈreɪ.təs
the means by which something operates; a collection of instruments or equipment

applicable adj
əˈplɪk.ə.bəl
relevant or appropriate; able to be applied

apparent adjective
əˈpær.ənt
readily seen or obvious; seeming

✏️ First check

A Circle the nouns in this list.

alleviate   arbitrary   apparatus   ambiguity   apparent

B Select a word from the ten key terms to match each definition.

related to chance _____

appropriate _____

uncertainty _____

obvious _____

C Underline the terms that are misspelled in this extract.

The authors must try to avoid ambiguty by producing a clear title. Amendments will therefore need to be made to the first two titles. The third title could, argaubly, be interpreted as both advocating and condoning the policy. The authors do alledge that titles submitted to this journal are often informal; this is apparant in their selection.

Second stage: Collocations and usage

Allege is a regular verb. Its past participle is **alleged** and its present participle is **alleging**. It has a related noun form, **allegation**.

> **Better than** say, reckon, believe

The reports often allege that spending is up on the previous year.

Usage notes: The main consideration for using the verb allege is that the claim is made without any real proof, or at least not that the wider public has witnessed or been given.

Farah and Ali (2016) allege that their machine is nearly twice as powerful as the M5.

When employed before the noun as a modifier, the past participle often refers to incidents and especially negative situations.

The alleged incident was said to have taken place in a government building.

Alleviate is a regular verb. Its past participle is alleviated and its present participle is alleviating. It has a related noun form, alleviation.

Better than make better, improve

Alleviate is often used after the following phrases: 'help(s) to', 'is designed to', 'does little to', 'does nothing to'.

Unfortunately, the decision does nothing to alleviate the burden on these people in the short term.

Usage notes: Alleviate is an appropriate choice for situations relating to concerns, symptoms, fears, effects, and burdens. 'Assuage' comes across a bit too expressive and whimsical for most academic situations, and 'abate' is restricted to certain contexts.

This was designed to alleviate the concerns of the residents.

The past participle is usually employed for instruction (with 'by') but is rarely used before a noun.

It can be alleviated by reducing caffeine intake.

Allocate is a regular verb. Its past participle is allocated and present participle is allocating. It has a related noun form, allocation.

Better than give, share

Allocate is used with three prepositions: 'for', 'to', and 'among'.

We will allocate this time for testing and refining.

These resources will be allocated to the departments involved in costing the scheme.

Allocate is commonly used with the nouns 'resources', 'time', and 'services'.

A key consideration was whether we could allocate sufficient time for this to be done.

Ambiguity is a noun that can be countable and uncountable. It has a related adjective form, **ambiguous**.

Better than vagueness, doubt

Singh and Sharma (2015) point out another ambiguity in the report.

Ambiguity is used with the verbs 'avoid', 'reduce', and 'remove/eliminate'. It commonly occurs with the quantity terms 'more', 'less', and 'greater'. Writers may also discuss the 'level of' ambiguity of something.

They need to eliminate the ambiguity in the admission criteria.

Usage notes: The first example referencing Singh and Sharma shows the countable use of the noun and a specific instance. More commonly, the noun is used in an uncountable way to show the need to prevent problems and confusion in general.

The checks are made at this stage to avoid ambiguity in the questions.

Amendment is a countable noun with a related verb form, **amend**.

Better than change, difference

It also affords the opportunity to make any necessary amendments.

Amendment is used with a number of verbs. These include: 'accept', 'adopt', 'approve'; 'oppose', 'reject', and 'withdraw'; 'draft', 'introduce' and 'make', and 'propose', 'suggest'.

All these amendments were opposed by the project manager.

The ministry would usually suggest some amendments to these proposals.

Apparatus is a noun that can be both countable and uncountable.

Better than gear, equipment, arrangement, way, practice

They considered corruption the illegal use of public apparatus for personal gain.

Apparatus is often modified by the adjectives 'security', 'state', and 'legal'.

This justice model is seen as an important part of the state apparatus for social control.

Usage notes: Although technically both countable and uncountable, the plural form is inelegant; when a distinction needs to be made, writers usually opt for quantity phrases such as 'a piece of' or 'a type of'.

Table 5.5 lists the types of apparatus used in each experiment.

The two general meanings of the noun are a physical piece of equipment (*a breathing apparatus*) and a system or method (*the apparatus of government*).

Apparent   is an adjective that can be used directly before a noun to modify it (*apparent problem*) or after a linking verb (*remains apparent*).

Better than obvious, noticeable

Nevertheless, it is apparent that the government has been moving slowly in that direction.

Apparent is mainly associated with 'become', 'now', and 'not'.

It was not apparent who was making the decisions in the company.

As a modifier (before the noun), its combinations are numerous, but quite often the phrase has a negative connotation.

The apparent difficulties mainly related to the complexity of the IT system.

Usage notes: This is another term that suffers from unnecessary adverb use. Avoid the common practice of placing 'very', 'easily', and 'strongly' before the term. The adverb 'apparently' is a related term when the meaning is 'seeming' but not when the meaning of the adjective is 'readily seen or obvious'. The former definition (usually when acting as a modifier 'the apparent issue') implies some doubt, whereas the latter (with a linking verb, *It is apparent...*) implies certainty.

Applicable   is an adjective that can be used directly before a noun to modify it (*applicable measures*) or after a linking verb (*become applicable*). It has a related verb form, **apply**.

Better than for, related, correct

This should be considered an exception and applicable only to oil exporting countries.

Applicable takes the prepositions 'to' and 'for'. It is used with the former when naming a person or subject and the latter for a period of time.

These strict guidelines were only applicable to members of the board.

The offer was applicable for three weeks.

Usage notes: The use of applicable immediately before a noun is usually for legal or financial purposes (*the applicable law, the applicable amount*).

Arbitrary

is an adjective that can be used directly before a noun to modify it (*arbitrary value*) or after a linking verb (*appears arbitrary*). It has a related adverb form, arbitrarily.

> **Better than** chance, random, guess

The theory depends on them making arbitrary decisions on these prices.

Arbitrary often modifies the nouns 'value', 'scale', 'judgement', and 'decision'.

The next step is to insert an arbitrary value into the system to check it works.

Arguably

is an adverb that often occurs after the verb 'to be'. It can also be employed as a sentence adverb (see 24) at the start of a sentence. It has a related adjective form, arguable.

> **Better than** probably, likely, perhaps

This is arguably the most difficult decision a guardian has to make.

Arguably, it was the introduction of a third entrance that caused this to happen.

Arguably can be used before the phrases 'the most', the least', 'the best', etc.

It was arguably the least surprising policy given the economic situation in the country.

Usage notes: Care must be taken when interpreting the adjective form (*arguable*) because it can be used for two purposes. The first relates to something being debatable, questionable, or unproven (usually with 'whether').

It is arguable whether the system worked as effectively as reported.

The second is similar in meaning to the adverb, that something could be the case.

While it is arguable that the government should be making these statements, the timing was unfortunate.

📋 Second check

A Which of the ten key terms do these synonyms relate to?

seeming, clear   _____

random, coincidental   _____

ease, lessen   _____

change, correction   _____

B Replace the struck-through word with a word from the ten available.

Once the ~~change~~ _____ was made the two parties could then reapply.

The difference between the two images was ~~there~~ _____ .

A study of the political ~~workings~~ _____ could indicate why these changes occurred.

Morgan and Jones (2009) ~~think~~ _____ that Fonseca had no way of knowing this.

C Select an appropriate option to match the key term.

This could be applicable to/with/of any of the staff in the building.

It is important to note the kind of/level of/size of ambiguity that each question produced.

These were allocated through/among/during the four groups.

3

articulate assert assign assumption attain attribute authentic beneficial capability characteristic

First stage: Introducing the terms

assumption   noun
ə'sʌmp.ʃən
taking something for granted or taking something as true without proof

articulate   verb
ɑː'tɪk.jə.leɪt
to express clearly and coherently in words

authentic   adjective
ɔː'θen.tɪk
genuine; reliable; historically accurate

characteristic   adj
ək.tə'rɪs.tɪk
typical of a thing or person; a distinctive quality

capability   noun
ˌkeɪ.pə'bɪl.ə.ti
the ability of something

Our original **assumption** was that they found it difficult to **articulate** the problems they were having. Indeed, the low **capability** of the students to interpret the **authentic** texts was **characteristic** of the participants that had been **assigned** to the first group. Many would **attribute** this to the colloquial nature of the texts. Researchers such as Singh (2004) have also **asserted** that, in order to **attain** comparable results, it would be **beneficial** if a vocabulary list with definitions was provided.

assign   verb
ə'saɪn
to select or allocate; to give out as a task or appoint to a role

attribute   verb
ə'trɪb.juːt
to regard as belonging to or resulting from

assert   verb
ə'sɜːt
to state with confidence; to maintain or insist

attain   verb
ə'teɪn
to achieve or accomplish; to reach or arrive at

beneficial   adj
ˌben.ɪ'fɪʃ.əl
advantageous; causing a good result

📋 First check

A   Circle the nouns in this list.

assign   beneficial   attain   capability   assert

B   Select a word from the ten key terms to match each definition.

to accomplish   _____

to appoint to a role   _____

to be coherent   _____

a distinctive quality   _____

C   Underline the terms that are misspelled in this extract.

It is benefical for learners to use authentic materials that have characteristics of real-life social situations. The learners in G2 attaining scores of higher than six can be atributed to the prolonged exposure they received to these materials, the assumption being that they had learnt more phrases and patterns than G1 and could employ them in the test.

Second stage: Collocations and usage

Articulate   is a regular verb. Its past participle is articulated and present participle is articulating. It has a related adjective form, articulate, and a related noun, articulation.

> **Better than** clearly speak, say

We only selected international workers who could articulate to the researchers what was actually taking place.

Articulate is used with a number of nouns including 'thoughts', 'feelings', 'emotions', 'reasons', and 'views'. It also follows 'help to', 'able/unable to', and 'attempt to'.

They were able to articulate their feelings on this matter once they began to feel comfortable in the environment.

Usage notes: Although the verb and adjective forms are spelled the same, they are pronounced differently: verb, ɑːˈtɪk.jə.leɪt; adjective, ɑːˈtɪk.jə.lət.

Assert is a regular verb. Its past participle is asserted and present participle is asserting. It has a related adjective form, assertive, and a related noun form, assertion.

Better than state, insist

Cham (1998) asserts that a participant would not be able to detect the difference.

Assert is often used in conjunction with the verbs 'begin', 'continue', and 'attempt'. It tends to relate to themes such as 'influence', 'power', and 'control'.

This was a time when they were beginning to assert their control over the industry.

Usage notes: The examples above show the two different uses of the verb. The first is as a reporting verb (*we assert/they assert*), and the second represents an action by someone that demonstrates power, control, or influence (*asserting their influence*). The reporting verb indicates that the person is confident in his or her belief, but proof is yet to be provided.

Assign is a regular verb. Its past participle is assigned and present participle is assigning. It has a related adjective form, assignable.

Better than give, name, send

They also recommend that at least three objects be assigned to each group.

Assign is often used with the numerical terms score/grade/value. Someone can also assign a meaning to something, importance to something, or a role or task to someone.

This task was assigned to the native speakers.

Usage notes: The prefix 're-' is commonly added to the verb to represent the action taking place again.

The three roles therefore need to be reassigned.

Assumption   is a countable noun with a related verb form, assume.

Better than guess, idea, belief

. . . the assumption being that they would know more about the company than outside investors would.

Assumption is usually modified by the terms 'general' or 'basic' and followed by 'that'. It is also used in the phrases 'based on the assumption', 'under the assumption', and 'work on the assumption'.

They worked on the general assumption that these alternative sources are still finite.

Attain   is a regular verb. Its past participle is attained and present participle is attaining. It has a related adjective form, attainable, and related noun forms, attainability and attainment.

Better than get to, manage, reach

The primary objective is to attain membership in this imagined community.

Attain normally relates to knowledge or skills, targets or success. It can also be used with control.

Many students use this route to attain the skills needed to work in the industry.

Usage notes: As well as taking possession of something, attain is used when something is achieved or accomplished. 'Acquire' (see 1) is similar in meaning but does not always involve effort or hard work (*They acquired this data from a colleague*). The related verb 'obtain' simply means to get something so also has a more general meaning.

Attribute   is a regular verb. Its past participle is attributed and present participle is attributing. It has a related adjective form, attributable.

Better than credit, blame

The party's support, on the other hand, can be attributed to more pragmatic reasons.

Attribute is often used in relation to success or failure.

Some scholars attribute this failure to the self-interest and greed within the party.

It can also relate to 'behaviour', 'changes', or 'outcomes'.

Fan (1999) attributes their behaviour to a lack of parental guidance.

Usage notes: The unrelated noun 'attribute' has a different pronunciation despite being spelled the same way: ə'trɪbjut, verb; 'æt.rɪ.bjuːt, noun. Again, be careful of unnecessary adverb use. Some of the more useful ones relating to degree are 'solely', 'largely', and 'partly'.

They partly attributed this to the early start.

Authentic

Authentic is an adjective that can be used directly before a noun to modify it (*authentic texts*) or after a linking verb (*appeared authentic*). It has a related verb form, authenticate (see 22), and noun forms, authenticity and authentication (see 21).

Better than real, true, genuine

They used an ethnographic approach to observe how people use this in an authentic environment.

Authentic usually modifies 'text', 'information', or 'examples'. Another common phrase is 'authentic experiences'.

These cultural visits provided the learners with authentic experiences that were lacking in the language classroom.

Usage notes: The verb 'authenticate' and noun 'authentication' mean to prove something or validate it and often appear in computer and communication fields; the noun 'authenticity' is used, along with the adjective, for sources and how well modern changes or interpretations correspond to historical ones.

The other users would then be able to authenticate this new network.

To retain its authenticity, a building should never undergo extensive restoration works.

Beneficial

Beneficial is an adjective that can be used directly before a noun to modify it (*beneficial treatment*) or after a linking verb (*prove beneficial*). It has a related verb form, benefit, and noun form, benefit.

Better than of use, positive

The beneficial effects of optimism among older adults have been extensively documented.

Beneficial is usually labelled with a comparative or superlative such as 'more' or 'most' and 'would be' / 'would not be' when evaluating.

It would not be beneficial to keep them longer than one hour.

It is generally followed by two prepositions: 'for' and 'to'. A choice is sometimes available.

This is beneficial to/for the company.

This is beneficial to/for their studies.

Usage notes: Avoid unnecessary adverbs such as 'extremely', 'entirely', or 'wholly'. Others such as 'mutually', 'potentially', and 'economically' offer more assistance to the writer and more information to the reader.

The terms of this latest contract were mutually beneficial.

It allows the researcher to view any potentially beneficial treatment programmes.

Capability   is a countable noun with a related adjective form, capable.

> **Better than** skill, knowledge, talent

These new dynamics can help develop capability by providing opportunities to gain experience.

Capability can form compounds with adjectives that describe certain fields or areas, e.g., 'military capability', 'technological capability', and 'intellectual capability'. It is often modified by 'limited', 'financial', and 'unique'.

They would be unable to match their rival's financial capability.

Usage notes: The uncountable form of the noun indicates general ability. The plural noun is usually used with 'beyond' or 'extent' to show the range of ability of someone or something.

Unfortunately, the extent of their capabilities did not stretch to time management and organization.

Characteristic   is an adjective that can be used directly before a noun to modify it (*characteristic functions*) or after a linking verb (*seem characteristic*). It has a related adverb form, characteristically, and noun form, characteristic.

> **Better than** typical, usual

Even after six weeks, some students were still making these characteristic errors.

Characteristic is used with the preposition 'of' when it is not directly preceding a noun.

These arguments are characteristic of board meetings in the company.

Usage notes: The noun refers to a feature or quality of someone or something, while the adjective is another term for 'typical' or 'distinctive'.

A characteristic that distinguished them was the ability to compromise.

These characteristic failings would also need to be addressed in the future.

📋 Second check

A Which of the ten key terms do these synonyms relate to?

ability, skill   _____

theory, belief   _____

normal, typical   _____

pronounce, utter   _____

B Replace the struck-through word with a word from the ten available.

The system ~~gives~~ _____ roles to less than half of the team.

I believe they have the ~~skill~~ _____ to carry out this task.

We should ~~link~~ _____ this to a lack of experience.

Half of the students had ~~gotten~~ _____ this skill by the end of stage 4.

C Select an appropriate option to match the key term.

I can see this being beneficial | in/to/with | both patients and carers.

They worked on the assumption | of/so/that | a new government would be in power soon.

These delays are characteristic | to/of/that | the way the department is run.

4

clarify coherent coincide collectively comparable compile complexity comprehensive conception conflicting

First stage: Introducing the terms

conflicting adjective
kən'flɪk.tɪŋ
being in disagreement;
not compatible

comparable adj
'kɒm.pər.ə.bəl
able to be compared; having
features in common; similar

collectively adverb
kə'lek.tɪv.li'
as a group or unit;
forming a whole

conception noun
kən'sep.ʃən
beginning, origination;
a notion; a plan

The company employed an IT consultant to direct the project from its **conception**; however, their previous work with a rival firm was seen as **conflicting**. After a meeting, the board **collectively** agreed that their own IT department would source **comparable** systems.

Due to the **complexity** of the system, the IT department took the decision to **compile** a **comprehensive** training manual to **clarify** the basic functions. This manual and a voluntary training course **coincided** with a company-wide launch in early 2015. The manual linked each activity to the department carrying it out, thus making it **coherent** enough for every employee to follow.

comprehensive adj
,kɒm.prɪ'hen.sɪv
broad in content or
scope; including most or
all; inclusive

complexity noun
kəm'plek.sə.ti
something intricate or
complex; something difficult
to understand or explain

clarify verb
'klær.ɪ.faɪ
to make clear or easy
to understand

compile verb
kəm'paɪl
to collect or gather; to
make something from
other sources

coherent adj
kəʊ'hɪə.rənt
consistent; logical;
harmonious

coincide verb
,kəʊ.ɪn'saɪd
to occur at the same time;
to be identical; to agree

✐ First check

A Circle the adjectives in this list.

coherent   comparable   conception   compile   collectively

B Select a word from the ten key terms to match each definition.

jointly   _____

logical   _____

incompatible   _____

occur at the same time   _____

C Underline the terms that are misspelled in this extract.

From concepcion to completion, the project manager clarifies the roles of each team member through a comprehesive and coherent handbook compiled at stage one. The next stage coincidies with the increasing complexity arising from the addition of multiple teams.

Second stage: Collocations and usage

Clarify   is a regular verb. Its past participle is clarified and present participle is clarifying. It has a related noun form, clarification.

> **Better than** explain, clear up, make clear

Because the experiment was not completed, further tests are needed to clarify these effects.

Often a writer will 'attempt to', 'try to', or 'seek to' clarify something. Sometimes something 'needs to' be clarified.

Writing out this procedure was an attempt to clarify some of its more difficult aspects.

The author also needs to clarify which ruling she is referring to here.

A role, thinking/thoughts, a view or point, and information tend to be clarified.

The group was told that they needed to clarify their thinking on this particular area of the task.

Usage notes: Clarify should only be used when something needs to be made clearer, usually because it is either inherently difficult or the initial explanation was inadequate. It should not be used merely as an alternative to 'explain' (see example below). To clarify is to give *more* details or a *simpler* explanation.

The teacher handed out the worksheets and then explained the activity to each group.

Afterwards, the teacher had to clarify the third part of the task and the role of Group C.

Coherent   is an adjective that can be used directly before a noun to modify it (*coherent ideas*) or after a linking verb (*proved to be coherent*). It has a related adverb form, **coherently**, and noun form, **coherence**.

Better than clear, understandable

The communication and cooperation guidelines enable all parties to work in an integrated and coherent fashion.

Coherent is normally used to modify the nouns 'message', 'narrative', 'explanation', 'view', and 'manner'.

In this instance, the writer failed to create a coherent narrative for the piece.

It is also used alongside the nouns 'framework', 'structure', and 'system'.

It is socially constructed through images that form a coherent system of non-verbal signs.

Coincide   is a regular verb. Its past participle is **coincided** and present participle is **coinciding**.

Better than happen at the same time, match

The country's independence and the subsequent declaration coincided with the onset of the Cold War.

It is used with the preposition 'with' and tends to relate to events.

It is important to ensure that it does not coincide with any other deadlines.

The phrases 'timed to' and launched to' are also used with coincide.

It was timed to coincide with peak availability.

Usage notes: The two main scenarios of use are for events happening either at the same time or nearly the same time (as in the above examples) and for two things being similar.

As long as their opinions broadly coincide, then the partnership can move forward.

Collectively   is an adverb that can come before or after the term it is modifying. It can also be employed as a sentence adverb (see 24) at the start of a sentence (*Collectively, they present a formidable obstacle to the inexperienced investor*). It has a related adjective form, collective.

> **Better than** all as one, together

One common strategy these enterprises use is to approach banks collectively.

Collectively tends to be used with 'act', 'represent', and 'examine'.

This volume collectively examines the economic and political outcomes.

It is also used before 'termed' and 'referred to as' when a group of things have the same name.

These direct, indirect, or incidental damages are collectively termed 'Damages' in the document.

Comparable   is an adjective that can be used directly before a noun to modify it (*comparable views*) or after a linking verb (*appear comparable*). It has a related adverb form, comparably, and noun form, comparability.

> **Better than** like, similar, able to be compared

In economic terms, luxury products are those that can consistently command and justify a higher price than products with comparable functions and similar quality.

Comparable is often used with 'data', 'growth', 'level', 'age', and 'value'.

They were of comparable age when first starting out.

It is used with the prepositions 'with', 'to', and 'in'.

It is comparable with/to earlier designs of the chassis.

They are comparable in size to the previous models.

Usage notes: Although the term suggests that the two things being 'compared' will be similar, they don't actually have to be alike; just one feature in common can make two things comparable.

The two regimes are comparable in the sense that they both failed to achieve their objectives.

Compile is a regular verb. Its past participle is compiled and present participle is compiling. It has related noun forms, compilation and compiler.

Better than make, collect, gather

First, the general analysis on data compiled in this research will be given.

Researchers and writers tend to compile 'data', 'lists', and 'information'. Sometimes the effort involved is measured as 'easy' or 'difficult'.

It was actually quite easy to compile the relevant information from the three sources.

The main issue is that it will be difficult to compile this data in the time allowed.

Usage notes: 'Compile' implies that some time and effort went into the action. It suggests more than just 'create' and is closer to 'accumulate' (see 1) or 'assemble'.

The author spent six years compiling the data from historical records and accounts.

Note that, as in the earlier example, when something is easy to compile, it is often surprising ('actually quite easy to compile').

Complexity is a countable noun with a related adjective form, complex.

Better than difficulty, complicatedness

For those products with low complexity, the effect is not as powerful.

Complexity is often measured by degree or level; it can be 'increased' or 'decreased' / 'reduced' or 'added' by something or someone. It can also be 'highlighted' and 'acknowledged'.

Munro (2016) added complexity to the second layer to resolve this.

It is hoped that these changes will reduce the complexity for the users.

They must also acknowledge the complexity of the other scheme.

Comprehensive   is an adjective that can be used directly before a noun to modify it (*comprehensive changes*) or after a linking verb (*This was comprehensive*). It has a related adverb form, comprehensively, and noun form, comprehensiveness.

> **Better than** large, wide, whole, broad

Kolb (1984) provides a comprehensive theory based on cognitive and social psychology.

The following nouns are usually described by comprehensive: 'approach', 'assessment', 'framework', 'network', 'programme', 'review', 'system'.

Colt and Morris (2001) recommend a comprehensive programme at this level.

The review of the literature presented in chapter 2 is comprehensive and covers the entire period.

Usage notes: Comprehensive is versatile and can relate to size, extent, completeness, and effort made.

The comprehensive report was an improvement on last year's half-finished version.

It was certainly a comprehensive examination of the topic by the team.

Conception   is a countable noun and an uncountable noun with a related noun form, concept, and a related adjective form, conceptional.

> **Better than** start, beginning, idea, view

Neoclassical realism presents a 'top-down' conception of the state.

Adjectives employed with the term include 'popular', 'broad', and 'common'.

He was considered to have a broad conception of democracy.

The preposition 'of' can also follow the noun.

This is the conception of privacy as detailed by Jeffers and March (1967).

Usage notes: Although there is overlap between the two nouns (conception and concept), a distinction can be made. A concept tends to represent a more general or widely held notion, whereas conception is the way an individual or group conceives or views/regards a particular thing.

The concept of citizenship is explored in the next section.

Their conception of citizenship in the country is presented in Figure 4.

Conflicting   is an adjective that can be used directly before a noun to modify it (*conflicting aims*) or after a linking verb (*are conflicting*). It is the present participle of the verb **conflict**.

> **Better than** differing, opposed

Public organizations have to deal with conflicting interests stemming from different stakeholders.

Conflicting is often used to modify the following nouns: 'interests', 'evidence', 'demands', 'reasons', 'views', and 'data'/'information'.

It might be that the display presented conflicting information and could have impaired performance.

Although these views are conflicting, they represent the two most likely explanations.

◻ Second check

A   Which of the ten key terms do these synonyms relate to?

jointly, mutually   _____

clear, logical   _____

opposing, differing   _____

thought, view   _____

B   Replace the struck-through word(s) with a word from the ten available.

The ~~idea~~ _____ of this particular piece centred on the stages of life.

The authors also ~~make clear~~ _____ that 0.500 is the limit only for the first two models.

A ~~clear~~ _____ framework is only possible if all departments work together to create it.

They have worked on ~~similar~~ _____ projects in the past with the same restrictions in place.

C Select an appropriate option to match the key term.

The *Conception* of/for/from *Winter* was a work by Maldonadi.

This is comparable on/in/at scope to the other databases.

The promotion needs to coincide with/in/to the beginning of the holidays.

5

considerable consistency consolidate constituent constitute constraint contemporary contend continuity contradictory

First stage: Introducing the terms

constraint noun
kən'streɪnt'
something that is restrictive; inhibition; a restraint

contemporary adj
kən'tem.pər.ər.i
belonging to the same age; occurring at the present time; having roughly the same age

consolidate verb
kən'sɒl.ɪ.deɪt
to unite; to make or become stronger or more stable

contend verb
kən'tend
to debate; to assert or maintain; to struggle with something or someone

considerable adj
kən'sɪd.ər.ə.bəl
great in size or extent; of noticeable importance

T-star **consolidated** its position as a market leader with **considerable** sales, despite the obvious **constraints** of a small budget and staff redundancies, which the sales team especially were forced to **contend** with. The **contemporary** design was particularly eye-catching and proved to be the **constituent** element that helped the product sell. The promotional material and accompanying designs further demonstrated their **consistency** in producing visually appealing modern products. This **continuity** was reflected by online sales that would **constitute** over 70% of the total sales, despite **contradictory** reports stating that online purchasing was low.

continuity noun
ˌkɒn.tɪ'njuː.ə.ti
logical connection or sequence; a connected whole

contradictory adj
ˌkɒn.trə'dɪk.tər.i
inconsistent or incompatible; asserting the opposite

constituent adj
kən'stɪtʃ.u.ənt
forming part of a whole; component

constitute verb
'kɒn.stɪ.tʃuːt
to make up or form

consistency noun
kən'sɪs.tən.si
agreement or harmony between parts or with facts or characteristics

considerable, consistency, consolidate, constituent, constitute,
constraint, contemporary, contend, continuity, contradictory

37

⚖️ First check

A Circle the adjectives in this list.

consolidate   constraint   continuity   considerable   consistency

B Select a word from the ten key terms to match each definition.

to make up   _____

component   _____

restriction   _____

to maintain   _____

C Underline the terms that are misspelled in this extract.

Many cotemporary critics recognize the contradictory nature of his work. Some contend that the constrains he faced in later life affected his technique, his etchings—constituting the artist's grey period—a prime example.

Second stage: Collocations and usage

Considerable   is an adjective that can be used directly before a noun to modify it (*considerable benefits*) or after a linking verb (*become considerable*). It has a related adverb form, considerably.

> **Better than** large, big, sizable

They will need to take considerable care at this stage so as not to disturb the subjects.

Considerable can often be found modifying 'amount', 'interest', 'time', and 'overlap'.

In the late 1990s there was considerable interest in this topic.

Usage notes: Considerable is certainly versatile and can be employed for size, distance, and extent. It is now rarely used to mean 'worth considering', only in the sense that it is technically being considered because it is so large or expansive.

Answers: A considerable   **B** constitute, constituent, constraint, contend   **C** cotemporary / contemporary, contraditory / contradictory, constrains / constraints

Consistency is an uncountable noun with a related adjective form, consistent.

Better than steadiness, evenness

Establishing consistency under such a system is a significant challenge.

Consistency is often used with the verbs 'ensure' and 'improve' and after the phrases 'lack of' and 'level of'.

We also noted a lack of consistency among the verdicts.

It also appears in the phrases 'consistency of responses' and 'consistency of the findings'.

These methods can be used to evaluate the consistency of the findings.

Usage notes: Consistency is sometimes used in the singular countable form (*There is a consistency about their work*), but the uncountable form is standard. A plural form is available only when the negative prefix 'in-' is used.

There were a number of inconsistencies in the description provided.

There was a lot of consistency during this period.

Consolidate is a regular verb. Its past participle is consolidated and present participle is consolidating. It has a related noun form, consolidation.

Better than join, make stronger

They use it to consolidate all the channels so as to optimize their performance.

It appears with the nouns 'power' and 'position', and 'learning', 'aims', and 'assets'.

How did they consolidate power during this time?

Usage notes: The most common meaning is to confirm or strengthen a position or an action.

The next stage was to consolidate the position of the college and develop links with the community.

Its other meaning relates to two things uniting or merging.

The idea was to consolidate the concepts into a unifying theory.

Constituent   is an adjective that is used directly before a noun to modify it. It has a related noun form, constituent.

Better than basic, main, major

Apart from Dar es Salaam, the university has constituent colleges in Uganda and Kenya.

The adjective is used primarily with 'parts' 'elements', 'data', and 'levels'.

There is a tendency for analysis to separate them into constituent elements, thereby losing the synergy.

Constitute   is a regular verb. Its past participle is constituted and present participle is constituting.

Better than form, make up

To clarify what constitutes a seaworthy vessel, Marshall (1998) offers this definition.

It is commonly used with risk or danger.

Even the smallest amount constitutes a significant risk to the host.

It is also used with percentages and fractions.

This constitutes 15% of the sample.

Usage notes: The examples above demonstrate the two uses of the word: the first being considered as something (*constitutes a risk*) and the second to be equivalent to (*constitutes 15%*).

Constraint   is a countable noun and an uncountable noun.

Better than check, issue, limit

Therefore, leveraged firms find it more difficult to raise external funds due to their financial constraints.

Apart from financial, the main constraint is 'time'. Constraints may be 'put' or 'placed', 'removed', or 'imposed'. Constraint is also modified by 'added' / 'additional' and 'potential'. The prepositions 'on' / 'upon' and 'within' / 'without' are also used.

This put additional constraints on the organization's ability to meet production requirements.

Working within the constraints of an SME proved difficult for some of the creative employees.

Usage notes: This noun is often confused with the verb 'constrain'. Ensure that the 't' is added for the noun. This is especially evident when the plural is required (*'a number of constraints'*, NOT *'a number of constrains'*).

The plural noun 'confines' is appropriate when referring to a boundary or limited range.

Working within the confines of the classroom makes it even more difficult.

Contemporary   is an adjective that can be used directly before a noun to modify it (*contemporary designs*) or after a linking verb (*sound contemporary*).

Better than now, today, current

Contemporary research indicates that more activities are involved than just the purchase itself.

Contemporary is commonly used to modify the nouns 'influence', 'works', society', 'issues', 'practice', 'model', 'debate', 'sources', and 'artists' / 'designers'.

Authenticity is believed to be one of the cornerstones of contemporary marketing practice.

Usage notes: Contemporary is just a more academic way of saying 'current' or 'today's'. There is an adverb form (*contemporarily*), but it sounds a little awkward and should perhaps be avoided.

There is also a noun form (written and spoken the same way) that refers to someone or something that was around at the same time as someone or something else.

He was a contemporary of the playwright Hong Sheng.

Contend   is a regular verb. Its past participle is contended and present participle is contending.

Better than argue, say, state, struggle

Working mothers contend with gender-based bias at the workplace.

Contend is often used to report what writers and authors have said.

Shah (2014) contends that a significant number will be needed.

Usage notes: The two main uses are illustrated in the examples above. The first is a struggle or problem that one has to put up with or try to overcome (*They have to contend with . . .*) and the second is to assert or maintain something (*The authors contend that . . .*).

Continuity is a countable noun and an uncountable noun.

Better than link, connection, uninterruption

Ward (2004) argued that, to ensure long-term success and continuity, owners must anticipate how current decisions and activities can influence the future of the business.

There is usually a 'need for', 'lack of', or 'sense of' continuity, and things can 'provide' or 'offer' it.

Critics pointed to the lack of continuity throughout the document.

The preposition 'between' is often employed after continuity. The phrase 'in continuity with' is also common.

The programme is in continuity with a previous venture led by the Anderson Group.

Usage notes: Opt for the uncountable form when talking generally (for instance, when continuity is desired or is a thing to aim for). The plural form is used for actual similarities or connections in an event or a system and within data.

Although Table 4.2 shows these continuities, we can explain them better in a graph (Figure 4).

Contradictory is an adjective that can be used directly before a noun to modify it (*contradictory reports*) or after a linking verb (*appear contradictory*). It has a related noun form, contradiction.

Better than clashing, in disagreement

Tozaj and Xhelilaj (2011) also listed the cases that represented contradictory precedents.

It tends to be used with the linking verbs 'appear', 'seem', and 'sound'.

The aims seem contradictory until you look more closely at the target market and their culture.

The nouns 'findings', 'outcomes', 'ideas', 'reports', and 'nature' are often modified by contradictory.

The contradictory findings of Cheung and Lam will not be taken into consideration here.

Usage notes: Contradictory does not always mean opposite. It can also relate to two things being incompatible or illogical, whereby if one thing is true then the other cannot be, or if one thing happens the other cannot.

The company profile was contradictory in that it claimed to have formed in 1987 and to have entered the Chinese market in 1986.

Second check

A Which of the ten key terms do these synonyms relate to?

insist, declare   _____

regularity, steadiness   _____

a check, limit   _____

establish, secure   _____

B Replace the struck-through word(s) with a word from the ten available.

~~Today's~~ _____ townscapes have designated spaces for this activity.

This ~~is~~ _____ a real problem if they spread further.

Most of the workers are just looking for ~~the same treatment~~ _____ with regard to disciplinary procedures.

These focus groups can often produce ~~differing~~ _____ viewpoints.

C Select an appropriate option to match the key term.

There is an urgent need to/of/for continuity regarding ownership of the company.

We soon recognized continuity within/through/between these two disorders.

This is a constraint of/to/on the ability of both the tutors and the assistants to carry out their jobs.

6

contributor conventional convey coordinate
correlation correspond culminate cumulative
decisive definitive

First stage: Introducing the terms

> **coordinate** verb
> kəʊˈɔː.dɪ.neɪt
> *to organize or integrate; to work
> together; to place in the same class*

> **definitive** adj
> dɪˈfɪn.ɪ.tɪv
> *conclusive;
> complete or fully
> defined*

> **culminate** verb
> ˈkʌl.mɪ.neɪt
> *to cause to end or to
> reach an end*

> **correspond** verb
> ˌkɒr.ɪˈspɒnd
> *to be in agreement;
> to be consistent; to be
> similar or to match*

> **conventional** adj
> kənˈven.ʃən.əl
> *conforming to or fol-
> lowing an accepted
> way or style*

The year tutor is charged with directing the teaching and ensuring there is a **definitive** plan in place. In Case A, the **conventional** structure whereby the deputy head is **coordinating** the teaching and having a strong influence did not seem to be **culminating** in success at classroom level. It was therefore hoped that smaller departmental teams would **correspond** to better communication and more **decisive** action plans—a **correlation** that the pilot study highlighted. The tutor should **convey** the message that all teachers are seen as **contributors** to the learning and the success of the institution. Studies have shown this to have a **cumulative** effect on motivation and morale (Moran 2001; Boorly 2004).

> **decisive** adj
> dɪˈsaɪ.sɪv
> *having the ability to make
> clear and definitive deci-
> sions; crucial; conclusive*

> **convey** verb
> kənˈveɪ
> *to communicate
> something; to transmit*

> **contributor** noun
> kənˈtrɪb.jə.tər
> *something that is a factor
> or partly responsible for
> something*

> **cumulative** adj
> ˈkjuː.mjə.lə.tɪv
> *growing in quantity or
> effect in a gradual way*

> **correlation** noun
> ˌkɒr.əˈleɪ.ʃən
> *mutual relation between
> two or more things*

📋 First check

A Circle the adjectives in this list.

conventional   convey   cumulative   correspond   decisive

B Select a word from the ten key terms to match each definition.

typical   _____

authoritative   _____

transmit   _____

reach an end   _____

C Underline the terms that are misspelled in this extract.

A major contributer to the field is Wenja Leung and his definitve model (Figure 3) conveying an emphasis on social customs. There is a corelation with the factors identified by Howson (2003), but Leung's model probably corresponds most to Lei's design of 2006 (Figure 4).

Second stage: Collocations and usage

Contributor is a countable noun with a related adjective form, **contributory**, and related verb form, **contribute**.

Better than factor, provider

Internal communication is another significant contributor.

Contributor can be followed by the preposition 'to'.

Tourism has always been the main contributor to the country's economy.

Adjectives commonly used with contributor include 'major', 'main', 'regular', 'leading', and 'likely'.

A diet low in iron and zinc is also a likely contributor.

Usage notes: The verb is favoured over the noun in most cases. The noun can be employed to provide a further example (*X contributes to Y; Z is also a contributor*). The adjective is a useful modifier and is often used alongside 'factor' (*Z is a contributory factor*).

Conventional is an adjective that can be used directly before a noun to modify it (*conventional stance*) or after a linking verb (*appear conventional*). It has a related adverb form, **conventionally**.

Better than normal, usual, typical

Category C represents the options provided by the conventional financial institutions.

Nouns that conventional tends to modify include 'view', 'method', 'technique', 'step', and 'role'.

This conventional view reflects the concerns of the central banks regarding economic instability.

Admittedly, this is not a conventional step but one the consultants feel will benefit the plan.

Convey is a regular verb. Its past participle is **conveyed** and present participle is **conveying**. It has a related adjective form, **conveyable**.

Better than say, mean, communicate

Whether the questions are translated accurately and convey the right meaning is another factor to consider.

Convey tends to be used with 'interest', 'information', 'a message', and 'meaning'.

The retailers in Thailand also adopted a variety of in-store advertising tools to convey key messages.

The adverbs 'accurately', 'adequately', 'effectively', and 'successfully' are commonly added to convey.

They successfully conveyed these ideas through conferences and interviews.

Usage notes: Convey is a good option when a meaning or message needs to be explained or is present or put across. For other situations 'express' is appropriate (*The authors expressed the view that three staff members need to be involved here. / The authors conveyed their enthusiasm for this interactive learning*).

Coordinate is a regular verb. Its past participle is coordinated and present participle is coordinating. It has related noun forms, coordination and coordinator, and a related adjective form, coordinative.

> **Better than** sort out, match, organize

The Ministry of Science and Innovation coordinates all the policies in this area.

Coordinate tends to be used with the nouns 'research', 'plans', 'approach', and 'services'.

Another staff member will be selected to coordinate the approach across the departments.

Coordinate is often followed by the preposition 'with'.

Each sector should coordinate with the national authorities when carrying out international activities.

Usage notes: When the general concept is required, the appropriate choice is the noun form. *The completion of a project depends on the level of coordination between these two units.*

Correlation is an uncountable and countable noun with a related adjective form, correlational.

> **Better than** link, connection

This reduced the power of the regression to detect any underlying correlation.

Correlations can be described as 'positive', 'negative', 'strong', 'weak', 'small', and 'significant', among other adjectives.

As expected, they found a strong correlation between unemployment and property crime.

Researchers can 'discover', 'establish', or 'find' a correlation, and a correlation may 'exist'.

They were the first to establish a correlation between risk-taking attitude and satisfaction with the business process.

Chan (2009) was unconvinced a correlation existed.

The prepositions 'with' and 'between' can be used after the noun.

Its correlation with the price of crude oil is also worth investigating.

There was no correlation between employee commitment and employee loyalty in their study.

Usage notes: Stick to the size adjectives listed above where possible, avoiding 'big correlation', 'great correlation', and 'wide correlation'.

Correspond   is a regular verb. Its past participle is corresponded and present participle is corresponding. It has a related adverb form, correspondingly.

Better than agree, match, link

Only ten social entrepreneurs agreed to be interviewed, which corresponds to a response rate of 25%.

Correspond can be linked to the prepositions 'with' and 'to' (see usage notes).

This relationship between the couple corresponds to that between Dante and Beatrice.

The number of users corresponds with the time taken to complete a security check.

The adverbs often used are 'broadly' and 'roughly'.

The beginning of the period roughly corresponds with the start of the uprisings.

Usage notes: As a general rule, 'correspond to' is used when two things are similar and 'correspond with' is used to represent agreement. The present participle is frequently employed (*These represent the slope coefficients on each corresponding independent variable*).

Culminate   is a regular verb. Its past participle is culminated and present participle is culminating. It has a related noun form, culmination.

Better than end, finish, close

The conflict within the party culminated in the 1980 election defeat.

Culminate is used with two prepositions, 'in' and 'with'.

The activity culminated with an identification of potential schemes for the future.

Usage notes: The past participle is rarely used to directly modify a noun (culminated + noun). The noun is often used in the form 'the/a culmination of'.

Cumulative   is an adjective that can be used directly before a noun to modify it (*cumulative score*) or after a linking verb (*should be cumulative*). It has a related adverb form, cumulatively.

> **Better than** more, adding, increasing

> *Buck (1992) identified that comprehension is a cumulative process and that early inferences lead to subsequent understanding.*

Cumulative is often employed to modify the nouns 'effect', 'incidence', 'records', 'risk', 'score', and 'loss' / 'gain'.

> *The company has never been profitable, experiencing an estimated cumulative loss reaching about 150 million euros in 1999.*

Usage notes: This adjective is sometimes confused with the verb 'to culminate' (above).

Decisive   is an adjective that can be used directly before a noun to modify it (*decisive action*) or after a linking verb (*must be decisive*). It has a related noun form, decisiveness, and an adverb form, decisively.

> **Better than** important, major, certain, firm

> *The SEA marked a decisive step in the development of campaigning on these issues.*

The verb 'prove' and adverb 'potentially' are often linked to decisive.

> *Their failure to act at the time proved decisive when the reforms finally came around.*

Nouns that are commonly modified include 'factor', 'victory', 'contribution', and 'action'.

> *Decisive action taken by those on the ground proved to be the turning point in the conflict.*

Usage notes: People are described as 'decisive' when they take firm action or make clear decisions.

What the company really needed was a leader who was authoritative and decisive.

Decisive can also mean that something is viewed as crucial or significant.

This was considered a decisive moment in the history of the institution.

Definitive   is an adjective that can be used directly before a noun to modify it (*definitive example*) or after a linking verb (*will need to be definitive*). It has a related adverb form, definitively.

> **Better than** final, best, classic

There are no definitive guidelines on how the training should be organized or how frequently.

Nouns that are commonly described include 'verdict', 'plan', 'statement', conclusion', 'results', and 'answer'.

The only definitive answer came when the interviewee was asked whether she attended the monthly meetings.

Usage notes: Definitive has two main definitions. The first is conclusive or final (*a definitive answer*), and the second is something that is the most complete, reliable, or recognized (*the definitive illustrator for Phillip Lam's work*). Adverbs should be avoided, as the adjective is 'definitive' enough on its own.

🗒 Second check

A   Which of the ten key terms do these synonyms relate to?

communicate, show   _____

key, final   _____

finish, conclude   _____

typical, standard   _____

B   Replace the struck-through word with a word from the ten available.

The ~~normal~~ _____ method lasts for less than 30 minutes.

Lack of foreign investment was also a ~~reason~~ _____ .

A number of the employees felt that the team leader was not ~~strong~~ _____ enough when choosing a system to implement.

This finding ~~matches~~ _____ to the opinions from the focus group.

C   Select an appropriate option to match the key term.

The merger culminated [to/in/from] the loss of almost 100 jobs.

There is a clear correlation [with/between/from] changing clubs and loss of form.

Otherwise, they could coordinate [on/to/with] the design team for a few months.

7

demonstrate denote depiction derive designate desirable determine differentiate discern disclose

First stage: Introducing the terms

designate verb
'dez.ɪg.neɪt
to indicate or point out;
to name; to nominate

depiction noun
dɪ'pɪk.ʃən
representation in image
form or in words

demonstrate verb
'dem.ən.streɪt
to show; to explain or
reveal; to protest

determine verb
dɪ'tɜː.mɪn
to conclude or ascertain; to
settle or decide something;
to shape or influence

differentiate verb
ˌdɪf.ə'ren.ʃi.eɪt
to distinguish
between; to change
or alter

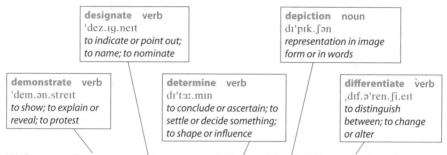

We hope to **demonstrate** that our model is capable of **differentiating** these two sets of learners. Recently, Lin (2015) **determined** that N2 learners have varying needs; he proceeded to **designate** five areas where specific and extended instruction would be **desirable**. Our own **depiction** of Lin's action plan (Figure 5) is also **derived** from Pinto's (2000) Structure of Knowledge. And despite our case study school failing to **disclose** how they **discern** these two groups, the fact that N3 students are fully integrated in the classroom **denotes** that these learners do have specific and unique needs and recognition of this is overdue.

derive verb
dɪ'raɪv
to obtain or trace from
a source or origin

desirable adj
dɪ'zaɪə.rə.bəl
worth having; attractive

denote verb
dɪ'nəʊt
to indicate or designate;
to have as a meaning

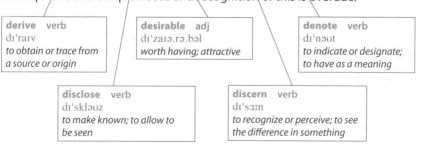

disclose verb
dɪ'skləʊz
to make known; to allow to
be seen

discern verb
dɪ'sɜːn
to recognize or perceive; to see
the difference in something

📋 First check

A Underline the verbs in this list.

derive   demonstrate   determine   desirable   denote

B Select a word from the ten key terms to match each definition.

to recognize   _____

to settle something   _____

attractive   _____

to distinguish between   _____

C Underline the terms that are misspelled in this extract.

McAdam and Jones (2001) demonstrate this method step by step, but a depicton of their system designating the points at which feedback occurs would have been desireable. We can determine three of the ten loops, but differentating the others proved problematic.

Second stage: Collocations and usage

Demonstrate   is a regular verb. Its past participle is demonstrated and present participle is demonstrating. It has a related noun form, demonstration.

> **Better than** show, prove, explain

Hans and Marks (1988) demonstrated this placebo effect in a study of patients with mild anxiety.

Demonstrate is used with nouns such as 'skill', 'ability', 'knowledge', and 'understanding'.

Section four allows the learners to demonstrate this knowledge.

Usage notes: Writers tend to be drawn to adverbs such as clearly, convincingly, and successfully where this verb is concerned. Only 'further demonstrates' has any real merit because something either does demonstrate or does not.

Answers: A derive, demonstrate, determine, denote   **B** discern, determine, desirable, differentiate   **C** depicton / depiction, desireable / desirable, differentating / differentiating

Denote   is a regular verb. Its past participle is denoted and present participle is denoting.

Better than mean, stand for

Bryman (2008: 296) denotes that secondary analysis is a good alternative for those with limited time and budget.

Denote is used for equations and nomenclature where a letter or symbol stands for a number, value, or name of something.

Domain, Dynamic, and Method Knowledge are denoted by D, Y, and M, respectively.

Usage notes: Denote tends to identify or indicate something (*This denotes the importance of each variable*). Designate gives a name to something or identifies a role for someone (*This period has been designated as the 'rebuilding phase' / They have been designated team leader for this task*).

Depiction   is an uncountable and a countable noun with a related verb form, depict.

Better than drawing, sketch, description

What emerges from Yaki (2001) is a depiction of the MPT as a ministry with limited power and influence.

A depiction can be described as 'accurate', 'exaggerated', or 'truthful'. It may also be 'famous' or 'modern'. Depiction is followed by the preposition 'of'.

The work is considered an accurate depiction of life at the time.

Usage notes: Consider whether the adjectives/adverbs 'graphical/graphically' and 'visual/visually' need to be added to the noun/verb if an actual figure or image is being presented (*This is depicted graphically in Figure 7*). Often 'depiction/depict' on its own is sufficient. Using these terms in a general discussion, though, is fine.

In the previous report, these statistics were depicted graphically.

Derive   is a regular verb. Its past participle is derived and present participle is deriving. It has a related adjective form, derivable.

Better than come from, related to

ADF tests assess the model derived from the AR (n) process.

Derive is often used with the nouns 'meaning', 'power', and 'benefits'.

These learners may not derive any meaning from this experiment.

Derive is followed by the preposition 'from'.

This meaning has been derived from many sources.

We derive this from the code written at the time as presented in Appendix IV.

Designate

is a regular verb. Its past participle is designated and present participle is designating. It has a related noun form, designator.

Better than call, name, show, point out

This newly formed organization was designated the promoter of ethical education.

These markings have been provided to designate the areas in which the activity can take place.

The past participle is often used with the preposition 'for'.

The area has been designated for students only.

Usage notes: Designate tends to give a name to something or identify a role for someone (*This period has been designated as the 'rebuilding phase'* / *They have been designated team leader for this task*). Denote merely identifies or indicates something (*This denotes the importance of each variable*).

Desirable

is an adjective that can be used directly before a noun to modify it (*desirable outcome*) or after a linking verb (*would be desirable*). It has a related adverb form, desirably, and noun form, desirability.

Better than needed, sought after, wanted

Others believe it is desirable to have the question preview in all standard listening comprehension tests.

Things can be 'seen', 'considered', 'deemed', and 'regarded' as desirable or 'become' desirable.

This career was regarded as desirable in the early part of the decade.

Desirable is used to describe the nouns 'outcome', 'situation', 'location', and 'solution'.

The parties met the following week, hoping for a desirable solution to the problem.

Common adverbs that precede the adjective include 'highly' and 'equally'.

Property in this region is also now highly desirable.

Usage notes: Desirable is quite a casual wish in the sense that if something is desirable, you may want it but you may not be working that hard to get it; for instance, *'50 participants would be desirable'* is more in hope and a pleasing outcome, but *'50 participants are required'* implies that only 50 will do and you will make a real effort to get 50.

Determine   is a regular verb. Its past participle is determined and present participle is determining.

> **Better than** work out, find out, fix

This method will help to determine the degree of significance and the quantitative relationships between variables.

Things can be easy, hard, difficult, possible, or impossible to determine.

It would have been difficult for them to determine whether their changes had worked at that stage.

Often determine is looking at the 'impact', 'effect', 'extent', or 'level' of something.

Their main aim was to determine the extent of the structural damage.

Usage notes: There are two meanings for the past participle 'determined'. One is to work something out (*These figures have now been determined*), and the other is being single-minded and motivated (*We could see that he was determined in everything he did*).

Differentiate   is a regular verb. Its past participle is differentiated and present participle is differentiating. It has a related noun form, differentiation.

> **Better than** separate, set apart, single out

Clearly, hiring managers need to differentiate between regular and outstanding candidates.

Differentiate is used with the prepositions 'from' and 'between'.

Small enterprises can therefore be differentiated from larger enterprises, using the previously mentioned factors.

We saw an instance of the pupils failing to differentiate between the two languages.

Usage notes: Differentiate is used for the distinction or the difference seen between two things. Discern is to notice or detect something. You can choose either in certain situations, but discern (see entry below) is often better for a difference that has been noticed visually and it will require an object, e.g., *They also discerned a difference between X and Y / They also differentiated between X and Y.*

Discern is a regular verb. Its past participle is discerned and present participle is discerning. It has a related adjective form, discernible.

Better than tell the difference, notice, see

They also discern the type of support that suits social enterprises.

Discern is often used with the nouns 'patterns', 'values', and 'differences'.

Some smaller species only discern this difference when they are threatened.

Something can be easy or difficult to discern.

With the system in place, it will be easier to discern when these attacks might occur.

Usage notes: Discern is to notice or detect something. Differentiate is used for the distinction or the difference seen between two things. Either is fine in certain situations but discern is often better for a difference that has been noticed visually and it will require an object, e.g., *They also discerned a difference between X and Y / They also differentiated between X and Y* (see previous entry).

Disclose is a regular verb. Its past participle is disclosed and present participle is disclosing. It has a related adjective form, disclosable.

Better than say, told

I would then have to disclose this information to the relevant authorities.

The most common things to disclose are information/data/records and identity.

It should be the 'duty' of the public authorities to disclose this information.

Someone might be 'obliged' or 'required' to disclose something or 'refuse', 'fail', or be 'reluctant' to.

This would only apply if someone failed to disclose his or her whereabouts at the time.

The preposition 'to' is used alongside the person receiving the information.

The welfare officer would then disclose this information to the line manager.

Usage notes: Disclose is a formal term for 'reveal' and is primarily used for legal, political, and business matters.

⌒ Second check

A Which of the ten key terms do these synonyms relate to?

drawing, illustration   _____

recognize, separate   _____

show, reveal   _____

come from, stem   _____

B Replace the struck-through word(s) with a word from the ten available.

The next step is to ~~work out~~ _____ which institutions should be used as case studies.

Although this would be ~~good~~ _____ , it is not essential to the success of the project.

The course leader must ~~pick~~ _____ which learning path to follow.

An asterisk (*) ~~means~~ _____ a wildcard value.

C Select an appropriate option to match the key term.

They must disclose these terms to/with/for the parent company before completion.

Most have been derived by/to/from historical sources.

It is probably the reason the depiction for/of/to this scene has been so popular.

8

discourse discrepancy discrete disparity
distinction elaborate elicit embody emerge
encompass

First stage: Introducing the terms

encompass verb
ɪnˈkʌm.pəs
*to include entirely; to
surround or enclose*

distinction noun
dɪˈstɪŋk.ʃən
*a distinguishing feature
between two similar things;
distinctive quality or qualities*

discourse noun
ˈdɪs.kɔːs
*verbal communication;
a formal treatment of a
subject or topic*

elaborate verb
iˈlæb.ə.reɪt
*to add information or
further explain something*

emerge verb
ɪˈmɜːdʒ
*to come into view; to
come out of something;
to arise; to develop*

The **discourse** revealed the **distinction** between the charity and the organizations studied by Peters (2001). From the interviews, it began to **emerge** that the title 'volunteer' **encompasses** more than just 'helping out'.

Participant B **elaborated** on this point when she revealed that 'even the volunteers **embody** this spirit and help us to reach more people with our fundraising'. One **discrepancy** was the efforts made to integrate the volunteers in the eastern and western regions. 'There is a **disparity** here. The **discrete** units set up in the west lack communication; therefore, volunteers may have a different experience depending on the unit they are assigned to.' Indeed, the eastern setup seemed to **elicit** strong feelings from the participants about the important role the volunteers play in this region.

discrepancy noun
dɪˈskrep.ən.si
*a slight conflict or variation
between things*

disparity noun
dɪˈspær.ə.ti
inequality or difference

discrete adj
dɪˈskriːt
*separate or distinct;
consisting of separate
parts*

elicit verb
iˈlɪs.ɪt
*to draw or bring out; to
give rise to*

embody verb
ɪmˈbɒd.i
*to embrace or express an idea
or principle; to be an example
of something; to incorporate*

✐ First check

A Circle the nouns in this list.

embody   discourse   disparity   elicit   emerge

B Select a word from the ten key terms to match each definition.

to explain further   _____

to draw out   _____

to arise   _____

to be an example of something _____

C Underline the terms that are misspelled in this extract.

A number of important points have emerged from the discourse, including the disparity between the managers and the employees. A distinction can also be made between the full-time employees and the part-time workers according to their outlook. The managers view some workers as not emboding the principles or the spirit of the brand, one elabarating that agency staff cannot be relied upon.

Second stage: Collocations and usage

Discourse is a countable noun and an uncountable noun. It has a related verb form, discourse.

> **Better than** conversation, work, talk, speak

One of the most important developments occurred in the 1970s through the discourse of neoliberalism.

Discourse is usually preceded by a type such as 'written' or 'academic' or followed by 'analysis', 'theory', or 'communities'.

The thesis aims to verify how beliefs about gender have been approved through written discourses.

Usage notes: Discourse is best employed to express the current debate and conversation occurring within a subject or topic (*The general discourse needs to move away from individual rights if any progress is to be made*). The verb is less common and should be avoided unless the writer has a firm understanding of where it would be appropriate.

Discrepancy is a countable noun.

Better than difference, glitch, problem

He also noted that learning only happens when there exists a discrepancy between what one knows and what one experiences.

Discrepancies tend to 'exist', 'arise', or 'occur'. They can be minor and slight or major and huge.

A slight discrepancy existed in the findings of both Sanchez (2001) and Diaz (2005, 2007).

Discrepancy is used with the prepositions 'between' and 'in'.

The problems include a discrepancy between the supply and the demand of the labour force.

Usage notes: Discrepancy refers to an inconsistency within something or between something (usually small), whereas disparity relates to inequality between two things (often large).

Discrete is an adjective that can be used directly before a noun to modify it (*discrete layers*) or after a linking verb (*should be discrete*). It has a related noun form, discreteness.

Better than different, unconnected, individual

As this is a discrete measurement that constitutes five years, it could be influenced by the previous factor.

Discrete tends to modify nouns such as 'categories', 'tasks', 'layers', 'units', 'methods', and 'skills'.

It involves placing products into discrete units and specifying activities.

> **Usage notes:** Avoid the common mistake of confusing this adjective with 'discreet', which means to be secretive and low key (noun form, discretion). 'Discrete' is often used to define data.
>
> *Discrete data is quantitative data that can be counted.*

Disparity is a noun that can be either countable or uncountable. It has a related adjective form, disparate.

> **Better than** difference, gap

> *This indicator is used to represent gender disparity in relation to learning outcomes.*

Disparity often occurs with 'increase' / 'decrease' or 'reduce' and 'wide' / 'widening'. 'Economic' and 'social' are used as modifiers, along with 'clear' and 'obvious'.

> *The literature shows there is also a clear disparity for those from socially disadvantaged backgrounds.*

> *They must address this economic disparity.*

Disparity is also used with the prepositions 'between' and 'in'.

> *The researcher argued that the disparity between what a student knows and what he or she encounters will be a shock to the student.*

> **Usage notes:** Disparity relates to inequality between two things (often large), whereas discrepancy refers to an inconsistency within something or between something (usually small).

Distinction is a noun that can be either countable or uncountable. It has a related adjective form, distinct.

> **Better than** difference, feature

> *This distinction might help organizations structure their recruitment channels.*

Distinctions tend to be 'made' or 'drawn'.

> *Rule 12 draws a distinction between decisions made by the department managers and those made by the board.*

The preposition 'between' follows the noun.

> *We can make a distinction here between the mainland and the island groups.*

Usage notes: Distinction attracts many adjectives. Only a few of them are suitable, and sometimes these may not be necessary. Common ones include 'subtle', 'obvious', 'crucial', 'useful', and 'clear'.

It is the subtle distinction between teaching the instrument and teaching the child to then interpret the music.

Elaborate　is a regular verb. Its past participle is **elaborated** and present participle is **elaborating**. It has a related noun form, **elaboration**.

Better than explain, go on, say more

She elaborated some significant information of her own to me.

Elaborate is used with 'ask to' 'attempt to', or 'refuse to'. The preposition 'on' may also follow the verb.

Most voters refuse to elaborate on their decision.

Nouns associated with elaborate include 'opportunity' and 'chance'; the adverb 'further' is also commonly added.

It also provided an opportunity to elaborate further on why the risks outweigh the benefits.

Usage notes: There is an adjective with the same spelling as this verb that means detailed or overly complex (*The planning was quite elaborate given the size of the task*). The pronunciation is different: adjective, iˈlæb.ər.ət; verb, iˈlæb.ə.reɪt. The adjective has a related adverb, 'elaborately'.

Elicit　is a regular verb. Its past participle is **elicited** and present participle is **eliciting**.

Better than cause, produce, get, bring about

The following themes and sub-themes were elicited from the interview transcriptions.

Elicit often follows 'designed to', 'attempt to', and 'help to'.

The questions are designed to elicit interest in the topic.

Nouns that form a relationship with elicit include 'information', 'behaviour', 'responses', 'meaning', 'beliefs', and 'praise'.

The student can elicit the difference in meaning more effectively using this system.

Embody   is a regular verb. Its past participle is **embodied** and present participle is **embodying**. It has a related noun form, **embodiment**.

> **Better than** stand for, mean

In time, a brand comes to embody a promise about the goods it identifies.

Embody is often used with the nouns 'values', 'principles', 'characteristics', 'elements', 'traits', and 'spirit'.

The system has failed to embody the values that the industry is built upon.

Usage notes: Embody is used much more regularly than the noun form (embodiment). It also has a more unifying and complete meaning of incorporating and expressing something than 'represent' and 'symbolize' have.

Through these donations, schemes, and charity initiatives, they embody the values of the company.

They represent the company at these conferences.

The number of managers that attended symbolizes the importance of this region to the company.

Emerge   is a regular verb. Its past participle is **emerged** and present participle is **emerging**. It has a related noun form, **emergence**, and adjective form, **emergent**.

> **Better than** appear, come out, occur

These associations emerged as top-down initiatives with bureaucratic designs.

Things 'begin to' and 'start to' emerge. These things tend to be 'meanings', 'ideas', 'themes', and 'actions'.

Once the group started talking, some common themes began to emerge.

The preposition 'from' often follows emerge.

Some strategic questions emerged from the conceptual framework.

Usage notes: Emerge implies a gradual or steady appearance of things; therefore, adverbs such as 'slowly' or 'gradually' are usually redundant. A comparable and equally effective term is 'materialize'.

Emerge can also mean something becoming eventually known (*It emerged that they had no prior experience in this industry*).

Encompass   is a regular verb. Its past participle is encompassed and present participle is encompassing.

> **Better than** include, involve, cover

The survey encompassed most of Hebei province and was carried out over two seasons.

Encompass is often used with the phrases 'a range of' or 'a variety of'. 'Actions', 'activities' and 'approaches' are commonly expressed.

The first module encompasses a variety of approaches to the problem of engagement.

These activities should also encompass many forms of support.

Second check

A   Which of the ten key terms do these synonyms relate to?

appear, occur   _____

extract   _____

difference, variation   _____

separate, unconnected   _____

B   Replace the struck-through word(s) with a word from the ten available.

The tutor would often *say more* _____ on why these movements became popular.

We also need to study the political *talk* _____ that was occurring at the time.

There is some *difference* _____ between what was claimed and what actually happened.

It was fascinating to hear the ideas that were *coming* _____ from the session.

C Select an appropriate option to match the key term.

This will only emerge on/in/from careful analysis of the data.

Newton elaborates more/further/extra in his third article.

It requires an ability to find a distinction between/from/in clauses that appear to be identical.

9

**endorse enhance enlist entail envision
equip equivalent establish exemplify explicit**

First stage: Introducing the terms

envision verb
ɪnˈvɪz·ən
*to imagine or expect something
to happen in the future*

establish verb
ɪˈstæb.lɪʃˈ
*to bring into being or create; to
install or set up; to prove correct*

explicit adj
ɪkˈsplɪs.ɪt
*clearly expressed or
demonstrated; unreserved*

endorse verb
ɪnˈdɔːs
*to give approval to;
to support*

exemplify verb
ɪgˈzem.plɪ.faɪ
*being in disagreement;
not compatible*

The trust **endorses** this new measure and **envisions** that all students will receive **explicit** instruction during the crucial summer period. This is **exemplified** by the 'Find your Calling' scheme.

Each college **enlists** an advisor who then **establishes** suitable paths for each student during individual sessions. These **entail** mock interviews to **enhance** students' understanding of the process and advise them on **equivalent** study programmes. The aim is to **equip** students with the necessary information to be able to make an informed choice.

enlist verb
ɪnˈlɪst
*to enter into something;
to secure someone for a
specific purpose; to enrol*

equip verb
ɪˈkwɪp
*to furnish with or
provide*

entail verb
ɪnˈteɪl
*to involve something;
to have as a necessary
consequence*

enhance verb
ɪnˈhɑːns
*to improve or raise
the quality or ability
of something*

equivalent adj
ɪˈkwɪv.əl.ənt
*equal, interchangeable or
corresponding; having the
same effect or meaning*

📋 First check

A Circle the verbs in this list.

enhance   entail   equivalent   establish   explicit

B Select a word from the ten key terms to match each definition.

equal   _____

to enter into   _____

to prove correct   _____

to provide   _____

C Underline the terms that are misspelled in this extract.

We enlisted the volunteers and equiped them with the enhanced devices. Establishing a link to the central control system entailed walking from the institution to the park, or an equivalent distance for the participants based in the other locations.

Second stage: Collocations and usage

Endorse is a regular verb. Its past participle is endorsed and present participle is endorsing. It has a related noun form, **endorsement**.

> **Better than** support, back, approve

Faculty members do not always endorse the internship programme, due to the lack of academic content.

People or entities are either 'ready to' endorse something or are 'reluctant to', 'unwilling to', 'refuse to', or 'fail to' do it.

They were reluctant to endorse a plan that had failed to consider the local residents.

Nouns that are used with endorse include 'recommendations', 'decisions', and 'strategies'.

The government has also endorsed these strategies in a rare show of unity with the institute.

Answers: A enhance, entail, enlist, equivalent, establish   **B** equivalent, establish, enlist, equip   **C** equiped / equipped

Adverbs that are used with endorse include 'publically', 'personally', 'officially', and 'unanimously'.

This has been personally endorsed by the director of the awarding body.

Enhance   is a regular verb. Its past participle is enhanced and present participle is enhancing. It has a related noun form, enhancement.

Better than make better, improve, add to

It is necessary for students to gain soft skills to enhance their employability after graduation.

Enhance is often in partnership with 'seek to', 'designed to', and 'help to'. Nouns that are used with enhance include 'skills', 'knowledge', 'understanding', 'performance', 'value', and 'level'.

The videos have been created to enhance their value in international markets.

Usage notes: The meaning of enhance has widened in recent years to also mean 'increase', but the most effective use of the term is to express something that has improved in quality, value, or desirability.

The aim is to enhance their experience when visiting these ancient sites.

Enlist   is a regular verb. Its past participle is enlisted and present participle is enlisting.

Better than use, select, get

In achieving this, I enlisted a qualified person to evaluate my inclusion and exclusion criteria.

People and entities can enlist the help/aid/support/services of someone or something.

Cranley (2001) suggests enlisting the help of companies in the industry to inform these hypotheses.

Often the people enlisted are professionals, experts, participants, or students.

The next stage involved enlisting students who had experience of working abroad.

Entail is a regular verb. Its past participle is entailed and present participle is entailing.

Better than involve, mean, need

Qualitative approaches usually entail formulating questions to be explored and developed in the research process, rather than hypotheses to be tested.

Entail is frequently preceded by an adverb. The possibilities include 'inevitably', 'necessarily', 'often', and 'usually'.

Therefore, this research methodology necessarily entails a deductive approach to find the relationships between the theories.

Usage notes: 'Involve' means to include or contain, whereas 'entail' can also relate to consequences and as such can be defined as 'to demand or require'.

This part involves selecting a number of teachers to participate.

This part will therefore also entail reducing the number of participants.

Envision is a regular verb. Its past participle is envisioned and present participle is envisioning.

Better than think, see, imagine

The document envisions that the higher education sector of Hong Kong will play a significant role.

Often, envision is preceded by 'begin to', 'try to', 'come to', 'hard to', and 'difficult to'.

It was hard to envision a more complicated first procedure for a junior doctor.

Usage notes: Envision is essentially a more academic way of saying 'imagine'. It does imply a sense of hope or desirability for something in the future, though. Imagine is more limited.

Equip is a regular verb. Its past participle is equipped and present participle is equipping.

Better than give, fit, prepare

The objective is to equip students with the basic skills to enable them to function as competent and productive citizens.

The nouns that tend to be used with equip are 'skills', 'ability', and 'knowledge'. The preposition 'with' should also be present.

The handbook was designed to equip the participants with the necessary local knowledge.

Equivalent   is an adjective that can be used directly before a noun to modify it (*equivalent salary*) or after a linking verb (*They are equivalent*). It has related noun forms, equivalence and equivalent, and a related adverb form, equivalently.

> **Better than** alike, same, equal

More firms are now able to provide equivalent or even higher salaries to attract Chinese employees.

The nouns it usually modifies include 'form', 'rate', 'score', and 'number'.

This will only be effective if an equivalent number of controls can be found.

Equivalent can be used with the prepositions 'to' and 'in'.

Their external debt was equivalent to almost 30% of the GDP at that time.

... although they are equivalent in size.

Usage notes: Equivalent does not mean identical but that something is essentially equal to something else in value, size, ability, etc. and is therefore a suitable substitute for it. For amount or numerical value, it is representative of it.

Establish   is a regular verb. Its past participle is established and present participle is establishing.

> **Better than** start, set up, begin

Fifty years ago, the Robbins Committee was established by the UK government to review the development of higher education.

A number of verbs can come before establish. These include 'attempt to', 'seek to', 'help to', and 'aim to'.

Some companies sought to establish links with the region even before the proposal had been drawn up.

Establish tends to be used with the nouns 'relationship', 'rules', 'picture', 'system', and 'base'.

Nicholls (1999) recommends establishing a picture of current practice before proceeding.

Suitable adverbs include 'newly', 'recently', and 'firmly'.

The newly established department took on 50 students to begin with.

Usage notes: Establish is regularly used to mean both creating or setting up something (*They established a learning resource centre the following year*) and finding out the truth about something or proving something (*Morgan (1998) established that this was true only for the adult males*).

Exemplify is a regular verb. Its past participle is exemplified and present participle is exemplifying. It has a related noun form, exemplifier, and adjective form, exemplifiable.

Better than show, give an example, stand for

These reforms exemplify how the different perceptions of the political parties can affect the national response.

'Themes', 'processes', 'stances', and 'principles' tend to be exemplified.

The model is going to exemplify certain stances that are desired by the employer.

Usage notes: Be careful not to write 'examplify'; also take care not to turn the verb into a noun ('an exemplify').

Explicit is an adjective that can be used directly before a noun to modify it (*explicit meanings*) or after a linking verb (*become explicit*). It has a related adverb form, explicitly.

Better than clear, obvious, open

There is no explicit model available for the chosen subject area.

Explicit often modifies the nouns 'instruction', 'guidelines', 'meanings', and 'guidance'.

At this stage, the learners benefit from explicit instruction.

Without a set of explicit guidelines, they continue to have only a very general understanding of company policy.

Usage notes: Explicit is a concise and effective way of saying that something is fully stated and clearly expressed so that no confusion or misinterpretation can occur.

✏️ Second check

A Which of the ten key terms do these synonyms relate to?

improve, boost   _____

involve, require   _____

show, find out   _____

alike, comparable   _____

B Replace the struck-through word with a word from the ten available.

It is unlikely they would ~~back~~ _____ a candidate with such liberal views.

We were ~~supplied~~ _____ with all the knowledge necessary to conduct an interview of this nature.

Learning a variety of social media tools can ~~improve~~ _____ their ability to communicate beyond the village.

He ~~imagined~~ _____ a design that would not require artificial materials.

C Select an appropriate option to match the key term.

This is equivalent | to/in/with | carrying five bags of sugar.

Were they equipped | to/with/in | the correct tools for the job?

The government will seek | in/to/with | establish a center within the next five years.

10

First stage: Introducing the terms

fundamental adj
ˌfʌn.dəˈmen.təl
of or serving as the foundation or basis; of great significance

gauge verb
ɡeɪdʒ
to measure or determine something; to estimate or appraise

feasible adj
ˈfiː.zə.bəl
capable of being accomplished; likely or probable

generate verb
ˈdʒen.ə.reɪt
to create or produce; to cause to be

functional adj
ˈfʌŋk.ʃən.əl
designed to be useful or practical; capable of working

I began by showing the assessment team some **functional** aspects of the model. This step was **fundamental** in demonstrating to them that my work would not only be **feasible** to use but could also **generate** profit. I **gauged** early on that the team was less interested in the physical model and more in the **exploration** of my design philosophy. They had already received a report that **formulated** my ideas and revealed the materials I was using to **facilitate** the environmental aspect. This report also included an **extensive** list of benefits that would later **frame** my closing argument.

frame verb
freɪm
to express something carefully; to plan; to conceive as an idea

extensive adj
ɪkˈsten.sɪv
covering a large area or great range

exploration noun
ˌek.spləˈreɪ.ʃən
an act of investigating or exploring; a trip to an unfamiliar area

facilitate verb
fəˈsɪl.ɪ.teɪt
to make something possible; to assist the progress of

formulate verb
ˈfɔː.mjə.leɪt
to express in systematic terms; to devise

📋 First check

A Circle the adjectives in this list.

facilitate   formulate   frame   gauge   exploration

B Select a word from the ten key terms to match each definition.

covering a wide area   _____

to assist   _____

practical   _____

to produce   _____

C Underline the terms that are misspelled in this extract.

One particular exploration that was fundamental to the topic was to gage the opinions of the workers. An extensive assessment of all staff data was not feasable for Li (2009), so he generated a smaller dataset of board members only. Specifically, the study was framed on the functional aspects of decision making by the board.

Second stage: Collocations and usage

Exploration is a noun that is both countable and uncountable. It has a related verb form, **explore**, and a related adjective form, **exploratory**.

> **Better than** look at, search

The stage I am at in my career is known as 'exploration'; hence, it is difficult to have a significant impact on my organization.

An exploration usually relates to 'themes', concepts', 'subjects', or 'ideas'.

This exploration of themes forms the initial stage of the project and is set to last two weeks.

It is used with the preposition 'of'.

Yin (1984) describes case studies as empirical explorations of a cotemporaneous phenomenon.

Answers: A None of them are adjectives **B** extensive, facilitate, functional, generate **C** gage / gauge, feasable / feasible

Usage notes: Exploration is sometimes seen in lists that detail the steps or stages of a study or its objectives (*step 1: an exploration of . . .*). The verb (*explore*) is more common, but the noun can be employed when a further instance is required to give variety to the text (e.g., *We will explore the reasons why the technique is proving so popular; this may also require an exploration of other techniques being practised*). This noun-verb combination is effective in academic writing and helps a writer avoid repetition.

Extensive
is an adjective that can be used directly before a noun to modify it (*extensive measures*) or after a linking verb (*should be extensive*). It has a related adverb form, extensively, and a related noun form, extensiveness.

Better than wide, broad, big, huge

Dr Tran has extensive knowledge on this subject and was therefore consulted at various stages.

Extensive tends to modify the nouns 'analysis', 'use', 'review', 'treatment', 'measure', 'list', 'reading', and 'research'.

An extensive review will take place if the profits are not as high as predicted.

Usage notes: Extensive should not be confused with the past participle of the verb 'to extend', which when used as an adjective (*extended hours* = longer than usual) means continued, stretched, or enlarged. 'Extensive' is less active in meaning and merely labels the size, amount, number, or degree (*extensive hours* = long).

Facilitate
is a regular verb. Its past participle is facilitated and present participle is facilitating. It has a related noun form, facilitator, and adjective form, facilitative.

Better than aid, help, allow

. . . hence, it was possible to facilitate the procedure and generate general discussion.

Nouns that form a partnership with facilitate include 'development', 'process', 'learning', 'comprehension', and 'understanding'.

The mediators were also present to facilitate the process.

Feasible   is an adjective that can be used directly before a noun to modify it (*feasible argument*) or after a linking verb (*This seemed feasible*). It has a related adverb form, **feasibly**, and a related noun form, **feasibility**.

> **Better than** likely, possible

The national policy should be revised to include feasible targets.

Feasible tends to modify the nouns 'way', 'approach', method', 'setting', and 'option'.

Over time it has proven to be the most feasible option.

It attracts many adverbs, but the most useful are 'economically', 'logistically', and 'scarcely'.

It is an alternative action now but was scarcely feasible at the time.

Usage notes: Feasible and viable (see 20) are similar in meaning, but a distinction can be made. Feasible is looking at whether something can be carried out, and viable relates to whether something can be successful or sustainable. Doing something might be feasible, but it may not be viable.

Within this timeframe, the project is not feasible in its current form.

Working with these small businesses for longer than a few weeks is not a viable option for the company.

Formulate   is a regular verb. Its past participle is formulated and present participle is **formulating**. It has a related noun form, **formulation**.

> **Better than** make, create, prepare

I will discuss the research findings related to each research question formulated in Chapter 4.

'Ideas', 'plans', 'opinions', 'solutions', 'questions', and 'theories' are often formulated.

Step 1: Formulate the research questions and set the objectives of the research.

The workshop is designed for brainstorming and formulating ideas.

These ideas and theories can be 'carefully', 'clearly', and 'specially' formulated.

Next time, these theories would have to be carefully formulated to produce satisfactory results.

Usage notes: Formulate has two main meanings: one is to express something in a clear or systematic way (*formulate your ideas*), and the other is to develop or devise something (*formulate a plan*). Arguments can be formulated or framed. When something is formulated it is created, but when framing something there is the possibility that more emphasis is placed on outcome and with a persuasive element involved (see entry below).

Frame is a regular verb. Its past participle is framed and present participle is framing. It has a related adjective form, framable.

Better than form, put together

Paradigms are practices that regulate inquiry by providing lenses, frames, and processes.

Frame is most commonly used with the nouns 'argument', 'discussion', 'question', and 'issue'.

Hewson (2009) suggests framing the questions, testing them in a focus group, and then reassessing.

Usage notes: Arguments can be framed or formulated. When something is formulated it is created, but when framing something the emphasis is on outcome and possibly persuasion. Questions may need to be framed in a certain way so as not to cause offence and to make them relevant, whereas formulating questions has a more general connotation of just creation (see previous entry).

Functional is an adjective that can be used directly before a noun to modify it (*functional needs*) or after a linking verb (*It has to be functional*). It has a related adverb form, functionally, and a related noun form, functionality.

Better than useful, usable, practical

These functional varieties of English are used in diverse sociolinguistic contexts.

Functional often modifies nouns such as 'use', 'purpose', 'skills', 'needs', 'unit', and 'approach'.

Morgan has taken a functional approach by actually looking at what activities these employees spend the most time doing.

Usage notes: Functional is beginning to be used in a slightly negative way to mean uninspiring and only fit for its basic purpose, or merely practical (*functional appearance*). But it can have a positive meaning as in the example directly above, where it implies a considered and suitable approach.

Fundamental is an adjective that can be used directly before a noun to modify it (*fundamental differences*) or after a linking verb (*This appears fundamental*). It has a related adverb form, **fundamentally**, and a related noun form, **fundamental**.

Better than basic, important

Identifying the period of responsibility is fundamental because the customers are liable for any damage or loss of goods during this period.

Fundamental is quite versatile but tends to be used before nouns such as 'questions', 'problems', 'principles', 'issues', 'differences', and 'nature'.

One of the fundamental issues in consumer behaviour is the way consumers develop, adapt, and use decision-making strategies.

The preposition 'to' follows fundamental.

Direct investment is fundamental to the success of the local schemes.

Usage notes: Fundamental as an adjective is usually used to mean key or crucial rather than its original meaning of basic or underlying, from which the plural noun (*fundamentals*) is derived.

Gauge is a regular verb. Its past participle is **gauged** and present participle is **gauging**. It has a related adjective form, **gaugeable**.

Better than work out, estimate, reckon

The measure used to gauge this opinion was selected after extensive analysis.

Often 'views', 'understanding', 'interest', and the 'extent' of something are gauged.

It is difficult to gauge the extent to which the ministry was able to shape policy in the early years.

Gauge is also used to judge the strength or power of something.

The instrument gauges the strength of the particular muscle.

Generate   is a regular verb. Its past participle is **generated** and present participle is **generating**. It has a related adjective form, **generative**.

> **Better than** make, start up, cause

As social enterprises aim to generate value, they need to continuously innovate, adapt, and learn.

Generate is often used alongside the nouns 'data', 'ideas', 'responses', 'codes', 'interest', and 'approval'.

We highlighted the key concepts to generate relevant data that could be explored easily.

These product launches always generate interest.

Adverbs that are used with generate include 'automatically', 'randomly', 'internally', and 'externally'.

The selection of the works to be used in the exam is externally generated.

Usage notes: Although it can have a similar meaning to 'create', generate tends to be more functional, mechanical, and methodical; create should in theory have an essence of creativity to it. Generate is therefore used a lot in the computer sciences and mathematics.

Second check

A   Which of the ten key terms do these synonyms relate to?

doable, achievable   _____

examination, search   _____

useful, practical   _____

wide, broad   _____

B   Replace the struck-through word(s) with a word from the ten available.

After this we will ~~judge~~ _____ how the subjects are doing.

This software has been chosen to ~~make~~ _____ our visual representations.

One of the ~~major~~ _____ differences is their ability to reason.

Are they able to ~~put across~~ _____ a considered opinion on these matters?

C Select an appropriate option to match the key term.

Section 12 is fundamental to/for/with the ruling.

Their next work was an exploration with/to/of conservation principles.

Pressing this button will automaticly/automaticaly/automatically generate a number between 12 and 25.

11

First stage: Introducing the terms

hypothesize (BE: hypothesise)   verb
haɪˈpɒθ.ə.saɪz
to give a possible explanation for something; to form as a hypothesis

incorporate   verb
ɪnˈkɔː.pər.eɪt
to put or introduce a part into something larger

inevitably   adv
ɪˈnev.ɪ.tə.bli
in a way that cannot be avoided

imperative   adj
ɪmˈper.ə.tɪv
important or urgent; required

implement   verb
ˈɪm.plɪ.ment
to perform or carry out; to put into effect

There will **inevitably** be opposition when **implementing** a project of this nature but Leung (2003) **hypothesized** that effective marketing is the critical factor. In today's society, it is **imperative** that a moral message be **incorporated** into advertisements, given the **growing** concerns about the dangers of these games. This was apparent from members of the focus group, whose **guiding** comments helped make our **implicit** message more explicit. The feedback also suggested that the **hypothetical** situations and their 'real world' **implications** could be a talking point for consumer groups.

hypothetical   adj
haɪ.pəˈθet.ɪ.kəl
supposed; assumed

growing   adj
ˈgrəʊ.ɪŋ
becoming greater in size or extent

implication   noun
ˌɪm.plɪˈkeɪ.ʃən
the effect something will have on something else; something that is suggested but not explicitly stated

implicit   adj
ɪmˈplɪs.ɪt
suggested but not directly stated; unreserved or absolute

guiding   adj
gaɪd ɪŋ
exerting control or influence; showing the way

📋 First check

A Circle the adjectives in this list.

guiding   hypothetical   implicit   implement   inevitably

B Select a word from the ten key terms to match each definition.

to put into effect   _____

urgent   _____

give an explanation   _____

unavoidably   _____

C Underline the terms that are misspelled in this extract.

Adams (2006) believes it is imperative that researchers incorperate current events into social policy studies. The growing opposition to these recent measures being implemented is therefore guiding our study; this trend is incorporated into H2, which hypothesies that its popularity has no influence on the government implimenting a policy.

Second stage: Collocations and usage

Growing   is an adjective that can be used directly before a noun to modify it (*growing concerns*) or after the verb 'to be' (*said to be growing*). It is the present participle of the verb **grow**. The related noun form is **growth**.

> **Better than** more, going up

Kuijpers et al. (2006) stressed the growing importance of career development not only for an employee but for the organization as well.

Growing tends to modify the nouns 'use', 'evidence', 'number', 'interest', 'conflict', 'call', 'consensus', and 'need'.

There is growing conflict between the two factions within the party.

'Rapidly' and 'constantly' are among the adverbs that modify this adjective.

The influence of these agencies has been growing rapidly since the 1990s.

Usage notes: This present participle is now being employed to describe all kinds of things. Make sure that it is NOT used with a noun that already indicates the same thing (*the growing increase / the growing rise / the growing emergence*). Note also that the past participle of 'grow' (*grown*) is rarely used directly before a noun in academic writing.

Guiding   is an adjective that is used directly before a noun to modify it (a *guiding strategy*). It is the present participle of the verb guide.

Better than showing, leading

Islam plays a guiding role in nation building and in fostering social harmony.

The nouns that guiding modifies include 'principles', 'questions', and 'strategies'.

These guiding principles are restated in chapter three of the document.

Hypothesize   is a regular verb. Its past participle is hypothesized and present participle is hypothesizing. It has a related noun form, hypothesis.

Better than imagine, think

Hypothesize is usually followed by 'that'.

We hypothesized that the following independent variables have a significant impact on cash holding.

Hypothetical   is an adjective that can be used directly before a noun to modify it (*hypothetical problem*) or after a linking verb (*but this is hypothetical*). It has a related adverb form, hypothetically.

Better than imaginary, unreal

The 'convergers' rely heavily on hypothetical and deductive reasoning.

Typical nouns that are modified by hypothetical include 'question', 'situation', 'choice', 'scenario', and 'problem'.

The respondents struggled to interpret the questions that were purely hypothetical.

Our case study looks at the hypothetical situation wherein the client fails to provide sufficient evidence that they have an overseas buyer.

Usage notes: A comparison with the adjective 'theoretical' would be useful here. Hypothetical means that something is either based on guesswork and assumptions or is an imaginary event or condition that has been created as an example. Theoretical is based on theories or ideas and problem-solving. It can mean that something is possible in theory but not necessarily in practice.

Next, we assessed the positive responses from the participants to the hypothetical scenarios.

This not only affects our theoretical understanding of reality, but it also has some practical consequences.

Imperative   is an adjective that can be used directly before a noun to modify it (*imperative clauses*) or after a linking verb (*This was imperative*). It has a related noun form, imperative, and adverb form, imperatively.

Better than needed, important

It is imperative to learn English to become a member of the global community.

Common phrases associated with imperative include 'make it', 'become', and 'remain'.

With the vote on the horizon, it makes it imperative that all potential supporters be regularly contacted.

It remains imperative to continue helping the well-funded sectors to reach their full potential.

Imperative is often followed by 'for' or 'that'.

It is imperative for students to engage with the tutors during these sessions.

Usage notes: Imperative is primarily used after a linking verb (*It was imperative / It appears imperative to . . .*). Avoid adding the unnecessary adverb 'absolutely'. The adjective is strong enough on its own.

Implement   is a regular verb. Its past participle is implemented and present participle is implementing. It has a related noun form, implementation, and a related adjective form, implementable/implemental.

Better than carry out, do

These roles will be implemented throughout the research study.

Implement is often found in combination with adjectives and other verbs as an infinitive.

Agree to implement/decide to implement/intend to implement/refuse to implement/forced to implement/be difficult (hard) to implement.

Nouns that are linked to this verb include 'change', 'plans', 'strategies', 'technology', and 'programmes'.

Gucci developed an immersive retail experience and would soon implement this new technology in all its flagship stores.

Adverbs associated with implement include 'partially', 'widely', 'effectively', and 'successfully'.

With government backing, this scheme was widely implemented in all schools in the region.

Implication   is a countable noun and an uncountable noun.

Better than effect, result, upshot

The implication of this study is to help managers better understand their employees' work life.

Adjectives that are linked to this noun either describe the extent of the implication (*'full'*, *'broader'*, *'wider'*) or the type (*'political'*, *'financial'*, *'environmental'*, etc.)

Prepositions associated with implication include 'of', 'for', 'about', and 'by'.

The developer must also recognize the findings and their implication for young gamers.

A second type that we will explore is defamation by implication.

Usage notes: Implication has two uses. The first is something that is indirectly stated or suggested (*The implication is that subjects with limited employment opportunities will be excluded from the program*). The second is the possible result of a decision or action, usually as a plural noun (*This has implications for several of the employees*).

Implicit   is an adjective that can be used directly before a noun to modify it (*implicit argument*) or after a linking verb (*was implicit*). It has a related adverb form, implicitly.

> **Better than** understood, hidden, total

Implicit vocabulary learning means the learner's attention is on the meaning of the message while listening, reading, or interacting.

Implicit tends to modify the nouns 'knowledge', 'learning', and 'argument'.

Implicit knowledge has been defined as the type of knowledge acquired unconsciously and naturally.

The preposition 'in' can come after implicit.

This viewpoint is implicit in some of the general descriptions he provided for the handbook.

Incorporate   is a regular verb. Its past participle is incorporated and present participle is incorporating. It has a related noun form, incorporation.

> **Better than** join, include, combine

The proposed Recruitment Framework incorporates culture as one of the key elements.

Incorporate often comes after 'how to', 'need to', and 'able to'.

We are not currently able to incorporate these features into our design.

It is used with the prepositions 'into', 'in', and 'within'.

All the information incorporated within this document is available on their website.

Usage notes: Incorporate implies adding something within the body of something else. Its synonym 'include' has a wider and more general meaning.

Inevitably   is an adverb that usually comes before the word it is modifying. It can also be used as a sentence adverb (see 24) at the start of a sentence. It has a related adjective form, inevitable.

> **Better than** as you might expect, without doubt

Inevitably, a few of the non-specialists found it difficult to master and ended up abandoning it.

Inevitably usually modifies 'result (in)', 'lead (to)', 'fail to', 'weaken', and 'spread'.

They do not believe that the biological differences will inevitably lead to gender differences.

A poor performance inevitably results in an internal review for someone.

Low doses inevitably fail to produce noticeable changes.

☑️ Second check

A Which of the ten key terms do these synonyms relate to?

showing, directing   _____

indirect, understood   _____

necessary, urgent   _____

assume, imagine   _____

B Replace the struck-through word with a word from the ten available.

With the ~~building~~ _____ pressure on the company to reveal its profits, CSR efforts become even more urgent.

The ~~suggestion~~ _____ was that few tutors would actually lead to more consistent teaching.

They tried to ~~put~~ _____ too many features in their system.

~~Obviously~~ _____, the reserve was overwhelmed by many of the invasive species.

C Select an appropriate option to match the key term.

This was incorporated | to/into/with | the project after the consultation period.

It is imperative | for/with/that | tutors to offer this support.

There is a wider implication | for/within/at | small businesses.

12

First stage: Introducing the terms

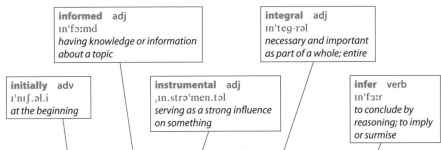

informed adj
ɪnˈfɔːmd
having knowledge or information about a topic

integral adj
ɪnˈteg·rəl
necessary and important as part of a whole; entire

initially adv
ɪˈnɪʃ.əl.i
at the beginning

instrumental adj
ˌɪn.strəˈmen.təl
serving as a strong influence on something

infer verb
ɪnˈfɜːr
to conclude by reasoning; to imply or surmise

Figure 3 presents the **informed** parties and their respective roles in the project. Song and Diaz (2009) have been **instrumental** in raising awareness of the main issues—private sector investment being **integral** to the success of these local schemes. **Initially**, prejudice **inherent** in the area was **inferred** by many to be the reason for the slow progress, but Mahmood (2011) **interprets** the poor outcome as a result of a weak strategy with no real **insight** into the local people's requirements; once the various factions **integrate** their support, they should be able to **intensify** their efforts and make the project a reality.

intensify verb
ɪnˈten.sɪ.faɪ
to make more intense; to strengthen

inherent adj
ɪnˈher.ənt
existing as a natural or essential part of something

insight noun
ˈɪn.saɪt
the ability to perceive the nature of something; a sudden understanding of the significance of something

integrate verb
ˈɪn.tɪ.greɪt
to bring together and incorporate; to combine

interpret verb
ɪnˈtɜː.prɪt
to understand in a particular way; to explain or clarify

First check

A   Circle the adjectives in this list.

inherent   initially   integral   intensify   interpret

B   Select a word from the ten key terms to match each definition.

to combine   _____

to strengthen   _____

at the start   _____

having knowledge   _____

C   Underline the terms that are misspelled in this extract.

The focus group helped to inform the second part of the study and was instrumental in shaping the interview questions. The interviewees were initally given some information about the project and then asked about their role, to gain insight into their experiences with the company. Their responses were noted and then intepreted through the IPret 2.0 software package.

Second stage: Collocations and usage

Infer   is a regular verb. Its past participle is **inferred** and present participle is **inferring**. It has a related noun form, **inference**, and a related adjective form, **inferable**.

Better than reason, reckon, suppose

We use this method to infer the value of investor protection in a cross-sectional sample of countries.

It is often 'wrong to' or 'reasonable to' infer something.

It would be wrong to infer that this tool is always available in the system analyst's environment.

Answers: A inherent, integral   **B** integrate, intensify, initially, informed
C initally / initially, intepreted / interpreted

Infer is linked with the nouns 'meanings', 'information', and 'relationships'. The likely preposition to use is 'from'.

The meanings inferred from these accounts have been represented in Tables 3.4–3.9.

Usage notes: Infer means to receive information and then to form a conclusion based on it. Often the information is vague, or the ideas have not been explicitly stated. The author of the information may have 'implied' something, which means that they have suggested something or made indirect statements from which the reader 'infers'.

Informed

Informed is an adjective that can be used directly before a noun to modify it (*informed audience*) or after a linking verb (*seem informed*). It is the past participle of the verb inform.

Better than told, learned, up to date

Informed consent was granted by each participant in the research at this stage.

Informed tends to modify the nouns 'consent' and 'decisions'. It can be preceded by the adverbs 'well' and 'reasonably', often together.

The employees were reasonably well informed about these external practices.

Informed decision making was another area on which to concentrate.

Several prepositions can be used with informed, including 'by', 'about', 'on', and 'of'.

This section will be informed by an extensive literature review on the topic.

Usage notes: Informed means having the necessary knowledge. It is either used directly before a noun to show that something is based on the required information (*informed decision* / *informed by* [something]), or with a linking verb to describe someone who is knowledgeable and perhaps cultured (*They desired employees who were informed and perceptive*).

Inherent

Inherent is an adjective that can be used directly before a noun to modify it (*inherent nature*) or after a linking verb—usually the verb 'to be' (*It is inherent in* …). It has a related adverb form, inherently.

Better than natural, inbuilt

This training should deal directly with core functions of the business that are inherent to each company separately.

Inherent is commonly employed with the nouns 'value', virtues', 'logic', 'nature', 'features', 'limitations', and 'danger'.

An appreciation of the inherent logic of the design was the main point put across at the conference.

It is used with the prepositions 'in' and 'to'.

This advanced search facility is inherent in every version of the database.

Usage notes: There is no real difference in meaning between the terms 'inherent' and 'intrinsic'. The only distinction is in the terms that writers use the two adjectives with. Inherent is the preferred choice with 'logic', 'nature', and 'danger', whereas intrinsic is more likely to be found with 'worth' and 'motivation'.

Initially   is an adverb that can be used as a sentence adverb (see 24) at the start of a sentence. It has a related adjective form, initial.

Better than firstly, at the start

Initially, the research aimed to investigate all five countries in the region.

Usually, someone initially 'sets out' or 'attempts to' do something.

We initially attempted to interview all of the students in the department.

Other terms modified by initially include 'intended', 'estimated', and 'reported'.

It was initially estimated that 50,000 workers would arrive over the next ten years.

Usage notes: Initially is used to introduce the first thing that happened or occurred. The adjective may be used to show the first idea, figure, stage or step (*The initial step was to locate . . .*), while the adverb usually explains what happened originally, before a change occurred (*Initially, we selected only female participants . . . but . . .*).

Insight   is a countable noun and an uncountable noun. It has a related adjective form, insightful.

Better than understanding, glimpse

Semi-structured and open-ended interviews will provide insight into these issues.

Verbs that are commonly used with insight include 'provide', 'gain', 'offer', and 'lack'.

The focus group discussions will allow us to gain further insight into the issues that matter.

It is also used with 'further', 'fresh', and 'unique', and the prepositions 'into', 'as to', and 'about'.

A unique insight about the way the firm operates in foreign markets was offered by Interviewee D.

Usage notes: The previous two examples demonstrate the uncountable noun (*further insight*) and the countable noun (*a unique insight*) forms.

Instrumental is an adjective that can be used directly before a noun to modify it (*instrumental advice*) or after a linking verb (*It appears instrumental*). It has a related adverb form, instrumentally.

Better than involved, responsible, vital

The study has been instrumental in providing a framework for understanding how the 'zero-poverty' policy has been adopted.

Often things 'prove' instrumental.

The second article proved instrumental in securing his legacy.

The prepositions 'in' and 'to' follow instrumental.

Assistance from the support staff will be instrumental to achieving the necessary level.

Usage notes: Although technically defined as useful, important, or helpful, instrumental is increasingly taking on a stronger meaning comparable to crucial or vital.

Integral is an adjective that can be used directly before a noun to modify it (*integral component*) or after a linking verb (*became integral*). It has a related adverb form, integrally.

Better than central, important, primary

Communication itself is being recognized as an integral part of each company, and their strategy in particular.

Integral tends to modify the nouns 'part', 'role', 'component', 'factor', and 'feature'. It is used in partnership with the preposition 'to'.

This is an integral part of the training and should not be avoided.

Evelyn, as the Head of Programmes, was integral to the success of our first presentation in New York.

Usage notes: Note the strong pause after the first syllable (*in*) and emphasis on the second (*teg*) when pronouncing the adjective: ɪn'teg·rəl. The mathematical noun term is pronounced slightly differently: 'ɪn.tɪ.grəl.

Integrate   is a regular verb. Its past participle is integrated and present participle is integrating. It has a related adjective form, integrative.

Better than mix, join in, add

These changes have given more opportunity for the departments to integrate with local stakeholders.

The adverbs 'successfully', 'effectively', 'fully', and 'easily' can be used with integrate.

We have successfully integrated this feature into our design.

Otherwise, there is no way to fully integrate the system so that all users can gain access to the reports.

Integrate is used with the prepositions 'into' and 'with'.

Next, we will integrate this into the design.

All of them are now integrated with SIMS.

Intensify   is a regular verb. Its past participle is intensified and present participle is intensifying. It has a related noun form, intensification.

Better than make stronger, build up, increase

Once the initial marketing has been completed, the interest in the product should intensify.

Intensify is often employed with the nouns 'effect', 'feelings', 'risk', 'relations', and 'pressure'.

The events served to intensify the relations between the two countries and ultimately led to the talks of 1954.

When these images were projected, it intensified the feelings of the viewers by up to 35%.

Usage notes: Meaning to increase in strength or degree, intensify is commonly used for human relations, emotions, debate, and political conflict. In the health and food sciences, it often relates to flavour or pain (*This ingredient should serve to intensify the flavour*).

Interpret   is a regular verb. Its past participle is interpreted and present participle is interpreting. It has a related noun form, interpretation, and related adjective forms, interpretable and interpretive (BE – interpretative).

> **Better than** understand, explain

They had the ability to interpret even the most complex of datasets.

Interpret often takes the adverbs 'differently', 'correctly', 'wrongly', and 'cautiously'.

This of course could be interpreted differently.

Diaz (2012) wrongly interpreted this to mean that the inner structure was not strong enough to take the load.

Usage notes: The two adjective forms are employed in different situations. The first, 'interpretable', means that something can be explained or understood (*Their actions are interpretable*). The second, 'interpretive', can be used to describe something (*These interpretative notes . . .*) or someone (*She was an interpretative artist who . . .*) that provides explanation or interpretation.

Second check

A   Which of the ten key terms do these synonyms relate to?

told, reported   _____

central, important   _____

to increase, strengthen   _____

awareness, perception   _____

B Replace the struck-through word(s) with a word from the ten available.

Morgan and Jones (2015) ~~suppose~~ _____ that these ambivalent charac-
ters were misinterpreted.

The company decided to ~~join together~~ _____ these three departments
into HR.

She was ~~really involved~~ _____ in ensuring that everyone reported these
incidents.

The failure of these projects only ~~increased~~ _____ the military's desire to
assert their control over the country.

C Select an appropriate option to match the key term.

They are unlikely to be able to integrate the components | to/into/from | the
model at this late stage.

The project manager was instrumental | with/to/in | choosing the regions to
cover.

Inactivity is inherent | with/for/in | every company and must be identified
quickly.

13

intrinsic magnitude manifest marginal
maximize minimal modify monitor
normative notably

First stage: Introducing the terms

manifest verb
ˈmæn.ɪ.fest
*to make clear or evident;
to show plainly*

notably adv
ˈnəʊ.tə.bli
*especially or most importantly;
to an important degree*

normative adj
ˈnɔː.mə.tɪv
*relating to rules or norms;
implying or creating a
norm or standard*

maximize (BE: maximise) verb
ˈmæk.sɪ.maɪz
*to increase to the greatest possible
degree; to make the most use of*

intrinsic adj
ɪnˈtrɪn.zɪk
*relating to the essential
nature of a thing;
inherent*

A **normative** standpoint in this respect may overlook the **intrinsic** value of change and diversity. It was Matthews (1998) who first **maximized** this variability by adding a third layer to incorporate the new ideas and opinions; **notably**, this layer was left unnamed but it helped to **manifest** the key concepts arising from the latest schema. Kohli (1999) also **modified** his framework, but the changes were **minimal**. He focused on the **marginal** issues of innovation and entrepreneurism. Yin (2009), meanwhile, **monitored** the development of these frameworks and noted the sheer **magnitude** of today's designs.

minimal adj
ˈmɪn.ɪ.məl
*of the least possible;
barely adequate*

marginal adj
ˈmɑː.dʒɪ.nəl
*at the outer or lower limit;
minimal or almost insuf-
ficient; insignificant*

modify verb
ˈmɒd.ɪ.faɪ
*to alter partially or
amend; to change the
structure or intent of
something*

magnitude noun
ˈmæg.nɪ.tʃuːd
*size or extent; great
importance*

monitor verb
ˈmɒn.ɪ.tər
*to check or watch closely;
to observe, record and keep
track of*

⏴⃗ First check

A Circle the adjectives in this list.

modify   normative   intrinsic   marginal   notably

B Select a word from the ten key terms to match each definition.

to watch closely   _____

scale, degree   _____

to show clearly   _____

being essential or basic to something   _____

C Underline the terms that are misspelled in this extract.

Given the magnitude of the task, the sample was modifyed to include only marginal groups. These groups will be monitered from a distance to ensure minimal interference; this will take place for at least six weeks to maximize the findings.

Second stage: Collocations and usage

Intrinsic   is an adjective that can be used directly before a noun to modify it (*intrinsic worth*) or after a linking verb (*This was intrinsic to . . .*). It has a related adverb form, intrinsically.

> **Better than** built in, natural

Where the purpose of an undesirable behaviour appears intrinsic, then the student must be encouraged to learn a different behaviour.

Intrinsic tends to modify the nouns 'use', 'part', 'value', 'reward', 'motivation', and 'worth'.

Critically, there are several intrinsic uses that have been identified as well.

Its intrinsic value is assessed differently by investors.

Usage notes: There is no real difference in meaning between the terms 'inherent' and 'intrinsic'. The only distinction is in the terms that writers use the two adjectives with. Inherent is the preferred choice with 'logic', 'nature', and 'danger', whereas intrinsic is likely to modify 'worth' and 'motivation'.

Magnitude   is a countable noun and an uncountable noun.

Better than size, importance, enormity

The degree of protection affects the magnitude of these managerial decisions.

Common uses include the magnitude of the 'problem', 'effect', 'differences', and 'risk'.

P-values fail to convey the magnitude of the differences between study groups.

They assess the magnitude of the problem that the government faces.

Magnitude is also used after 'similar', 'equal', and 'sufficient'.

Objects F, H, and O are of sufficient magnitude for our experiment.

Usage notes: 'Magnitude' is a sound choice when the quality of being large or the metaphorical size of something forms the discussion. 'Size' is generally used for physical measurement or dimensions.

They soon appreciated the sheer magnitude of these ideas.

They soon appreciated the sheer size of this device.

Manifest   is a regular verb. Its past participle is manifested and present participle is manifesting. It has a related noun form, manifestation.

Better than show, display

There are important elements of multilevel governance that manifest in these policy networks.

'Tensions', 'problems', and 'effects' often manifest in some way (usually 'easily', 'clearly', or 'repeatedly').

Substance use leads to health problems among these adults, but the effects clearly manifest at a later point for those in group 1.

The prepositions 'as', 'in', and 'within' are used with manifest.

The disease can manifest as episodic, chronic, and even fatal.

Usage notes: There is also an adjective form with the same spelling as the verb. It can create a rather awkward construction if the writer is just looking for a more formal word for 'obvious' or 'clear' and should therefore only be used if possessing a good understanding of the term.

Their anger towards these changes was manifest.

Marginal is an adjective that can be used directly before a noun to modify it (*marginal effects*) or after a linking verb (*likely to be marginal*). It has a related adverb form, marginally, and a related noun form, marginality.

Better than small, low, slight, minor

Figure 1 indicates that the marginal cost curve of liquid asset shortage is downward sloping.

Marginal is a versatile adjective but is usually found modifying 'impact', 'effect', 'increase' / 'decrease', 'benefit', and 'improvement'.

There was a marginal increase in satisfaction scores for group three (see Table 4-3).

Patients should expect to see a marginal improvement after a few days.

Usage notes: Marginal is more likely to mean 'insignificant' or 'small' than the physical or social sense of 'at the margins'. The latter definition occurs with the nouns 'group', 'community', or 'language'.

They surveyed three of these marginal communities to see how they have been affected by the government's actions on this matter.

Maximize is a regular verb. Its past participle is maximized and present participle is maximizing. It has a related noun form, maximization.

Better than make the most of, use to the full, increase, enlarge

This regional reform maximized the political benefits for the ruling party.

Most things can be maximized, but the common associations in academic literature include 'opportunities' / 'chances', 'benefits', 'gains', 'funds' / 'profits', 'potential', and 'efficiency'.

Dividing the area among the five members should maximize their chances of visiting every town.

Regardless of size or influence, the sole aim is to maximize profits.

Minimal   is an adjective that can be used directly before a noun to modify it (*minimal changes*) or after a linking verb (*will remain minimal*). It has a related adverb form, minimally.

> **Better than** least, smallest

It is naïve to assume that minimal exposure to the context would automatically reduce or eliminate bias (Rosa 2010).

Minimal can be used in many situations. Typical associations include the nouns 'losses', 'difference', 'changes', 'risk', 'effort', 'information', and 'intervention'.

The shareholders would expect to see minimal losses from a venture of this type.

The police were expected to make progress despite the minimal information given.

Usage notes: Minimal can have the meaning of very slight (*minimal effect*) or very low (*minimal standards*). As a comparison, 'least', a superlative, means the lowest possible among the things being compared (. . . *the least effective of all the techniques*).

Modify   is a regular verb. Its past participle is modified and present participle is modifying. It has a related noun form, modification, and a related adjective form, modifiable.

> **Better than** change, vary

The implication is that an inclusive school would need to modify or restructure these practices and this culture.

Nouns that are used with modify include 'effect', 'size' 'behaviour', 'lifestyle', treatment', and 'requirements'.

We must acquire, modify, and then reinforce this lifestyle so it becomes normal behaviour for the younger generation.

She was allowed to modify her requirements as long as they were submitted before the deadline.

Suitable adverbs to use include 'partially', 'slightly', 'highly', and 'accordingly'.

The task for the second group was slightly modified; they were given no final instruction.

Usage notes: Modify implies that a small adjustment, or just a few adjustments, needs to be made. 'Change' usually means major adjustments (see 1) or a replacement. Modify may be preferred to 'alter' for more technical changes, such as to a computer program or equipment. 'Alter' may also be considered to mean a greater degree of change, e.g., if you modify your teaching methods you make slight changes, but if you alter your teaching methods you take a different approach to the teaching.

Monitor
is a regular verb. Its past participle is monitored and present participle is monitoring.

Better than check, watch, look closely

They influence the extent to which the manager is willing to monitor and advise the staff.

'Progress', 'effects', 'usage' / 'use', and 'activity' tend to be monitored.

This also means their usage will be monitored for several weeks.

Many adverbs are used with monitor, including 'carefully', 'closely', 'strictly', 'regularly', and 'routinely'.

After the scandal, the company was strictly monitored and prohibited from taking on any new clients.

Normative
is an adjective that can be used directly before a noun to modify it (*normative method*) or after a linking verb (*remain normative*). It has a related adverb form, normatively.

Better than rule-based, norm-based

The research in these fields has a tendency to be normative and legalistic rather than empirical.

Normative usually relates to 'data', 'value', 'sample', or 'behaviour'.

They suggest keeping them in the normative sample to ensure that it reaches a sufficient number.

Usage notes: Normative is based on the noun 'norm' rather than the adjective 'normal'. Normal means habitual or usual; normative means a standard or a norm that is prescriptive and often based on ideal social behaviour rather than just common habit.

Notably   is an adverb that can be employed as a sentence adverb (see 24) at the start of a sentence. It has a related adjective form, **notable**.

> **Better than** especially, particularly

Notably, competitors such as Apple and HTC were hampering Nokia's performance.

Often the adjectives 'different', 'higher' / 'lower', and 'reduced' are modified by notably.

The scores were notably lower the second time, perhaps because motivation had decreased.

Notably can also be preceded by 'most'.

Performance was reduced after the completion of around 50 laps, most notably in acceleration.

Second check

A   Which of the ten key terms do these synonyms relate to?

to change, amend   _____

slight, least   _____

to check, watch   _____

at the limit, insignificant _____

B   Replace the struck-through word(s) with a word from the ten available.

The sheer ~~size~~ _____ of the project was an initial concern.

This could ~~show~~ _____ in a number of different ways.

With more effective planning they could ~~make the most of~~ _____ their potential.

The team deliberately focused on ~~core~~ _____ capabilities.

C   Select an appropriate option to match the key term.

This law is now beginning to manifest at/in/for the United States.

The profits for 2015 represent a marginally/marginal/margin increase over last year's.

We might have to slightly/steeply/minimally modify some of these designs.

14

First stage: Introducing the terms

outline verb
'aʊt.laɪn
*to give the main features
or general idea*

offset verb
ˌɒf'set
*to counterbalance or
compensate for*

object verb
əb'dʒekt
*to feel or express
opposition to someone
or something*

omit verb
əʊ'mɪt
*to fail to include or
do something*

partial adj
'pɑː.ʃəl
*incomplete; relating
to only a part; minor*

Most of the available reports on this tend to **outline** the **partial** relocation of the call centres but **omit** the poor performance of the last two quarters. Madison (2014) also **objects** to this idea that the management could have **offset** these losses by entering newer markets, thus giving the **perception** to the shareholders that the company is developing and that the director is **overseeing** a new era of expansion. It occurs to us that this **notion** of development and enterprise in a recession is somewhat of a **paradox**, especially given that the **optimal** conditions for this policy had occurred only nine months earlier.

paradox noun
'pær.ə.dɒks
*a situation or statement that
appears contradictory*

oversee verb
ˌəʊ.və'siː
*to direct, supervise,
or manage*

optimal adj
'ɒp.tɪ.məl
*best or most
favourable*

notion noun
'nəʊ.ʃən
*a belief or idea; a
general understanding*

perception noun
pə'sep.ʃən
*the ability or capacity to perceive;
the act of perceiving; belief or
opinion held by people*

📋 First check

A Circle the verbs in this list.

offset   partial   perception   oversee   optimal

B Select a word from the ten key terms to match each definition.

an idea   _____

most favourable   _____

incomplete   _____

to show the main features _____

C Underline the terms that are misspelled in this extract.

This perseption of failure is also outlined in Lam's theory. Lam ommits the notion of peer pressure but off sets this with a social attitude factor and a partail exploration of emotional development.

Second stage: Collocations and usage

Notion   is a countable noun and has a related adjective form, notional.

Better than idea, view, thought

Most parties embraced the central notion of national unity.

Notion is often preceded by 'vague', 'peculiar', 'romantic', or 'popular'.

This popular notion can be harmful to their motivation for learning history.

A notion can be 'supported', 'rejected', or 'accepted'. The preposition 'of' sometimes follows the noun.

The entire board supported the notion of keeping the schemes local.

Usage notes: Notion has two main meanings. It can be used for an idea, opinion or belief (*This notion of fate is quite flexible*). It can also mean a vague or basic understanding of something (*They had a notion of how this should be carried out*).

Object   is a regular verb. Its past participle is objected and present participle is objecting. It has a related noun form, objection.

Better than be against, moan, complain

They did not object to the scheme in principle, but a few issues were raised during the discussions.

Object is followed by the preposition 'to'.

The creator objected to the following alterations from the design team:

Usage notes: Oppose has a similar meaning to object but implies that action has been or will be taken. Object tends to be a verbal complaint. Modifiers such as 'strongly' and 'vehemently' are used before object but are not particularly necessary. If someone objects to something, it is fairly clear they disagree with it, so any adverbs could be considered unnecessary and redundant.

Offset   is an irregular verb. Its past participle is offset and present participle is offsetting.

Better than balance, counter

For the out-of-sample performance, the gains are offset by the estimation error.

Offset normally relates to 'cost', 'effects', or 'losses'.

These measures should offset the losses experienced by the firms.

The preposition 'against' can follow offset.

The monthly payments made by the company are then offset against their taxable profits.

Usage notes: Make sure that the term is NOT split into two words (*off set*). The present, future, past, and past participle forms are all the same (*offset*). Respectively,

we offset
we will offset
we offset
we have offset

Omit   is a regular verb. Its past participle is omitted and present participle is omitting. It has a related noun form, omission.

Better than miss out, skip, ignore

Owing to unavailable data, we had to omit Laos from the sample.

'Facts', 'data', 'words', and 'variables' tend to be omitted.

Errors in this study included words that were omitted when transcribing the interviews.

Certain adverbs are common with omit. These include 'accidentally', 'wrongly', 'deliberately', and 'conspicuously'. The preposition 'from' can follow the verb.

Some of the negative articles were deliberately omitted from the review by the researchers.

Usage notes: When something has been left out by accident or because of carelessness, 'omit' is a better option than 'exclude' or 'leave out' (*The reviewers also noticed that the researcher had omitted an important finding from the discussion*). It can also mean to leave out deliberately (*We omitted these details from the final report*).

Optimal   is an adjective that can be used directly before a noun to modify it (*optimal number*) or after a linking verb (*appears optimal*). It has a related adjective form, optimum, and adverb form, optimally.

Better than best, most favourable

Whether there is an optimal outcome has recently been a focus of attention in the empirical literature.

Optimal often modifies the nouns 'value' / 'number', 'power', 'level', 'conditions', 'efficiency', 'results', and 'growth'.

Nevertheless, the development of these special zones has not provided optimal results.

Usage notes: A distinction can be made between the two adjectives. 'Optimum' usually describes the ideal or best amount and is used in a more specific sense than 'optimal', which is based on circumstances and relates more to quality (*This is not an optimal solution because the energy levels are too low*).

Optimal cannot be used as a noun, whereas optimum can.

All parties agreed that the optimum would change from time to time. (noun)

Outline   is a regular verb. Its past participle is outlined and present participle is outlining.

Better than sketch, show, plan

Sub-hypotheses regarding how their interests were shaped were also outlined in this chapter.

Outline can receive the adverbs 'briefly', 'clearly', and 'roughly'.

We will briefly outline this procedure in the next section.

The position of the place something was outlined is also often expressed: 'above', 'below', 'here', 'next'.

The dissertation comprises seven chapters as outlined below.

Oversee   is an irregular verb. Its past participle is overseen and present participle is overseeing.

Better than run, manage

This new body is set to be an external third party that oversees higher education institutions.

Things being overseen tend to include 'matters', 'processes', 'systems' or an 'implementation'.

The Provincial Commissioners oversee the implementation of all policies on the island.

Adverbs connected to oversee include 'directly' and 'personally'.

The HR manager personally oversees the training that takes place internally.

Usage notes: Note that this is an irregular verb, and the simple past form is 'oversaw'.

Paradox   is a countable noun and an uncountable noun. It has a related adjective form, paradoxical, and adverb form, paradoxically.

Better than irony, puzzle

Their paper looked at the paradox in managing new product development.

A paradox can be 'posed', 'presented', or 'resolved'.

The writer presented the paradox of being famous and obscure at the same time.

Partial is an adjective that can be used directly before a noun to modify it (*partial support*). It has a related adverb form, partially.

Better than unfinished, half, part

Figure 5.3 represents the partial sequence of this RNA gene.

Partial can be used with a variety of nouns. The most common include 'list', 'agreement', 'recovery', 'loss', and 'role'.

It is evident that personal factors such as age, education, and nationality play a partial role in influencing employee behaviour.

The minimum aim is to achieve a partial recovery of the data.

Usage notes: Partial is primarily used directly before a noun rather than alongside a linking verb in academic English. Although partial can mean 'incomplete', the terms are not necessarily interchangeable. 'Incomplete' would not be used before the nouns 'loss' and 'role' when the meaning relates to small or minor. 'Partial' carries out this task instead.

One of the consequences is a partial loss of vision.

She had a partial role in the second experiment.

Perception is a countable noun and an uncountable noun. It has a related verb form, perceive, and adjective forms, perceptible and perceptive.

Better than view, opinion, understanding

This study investigated Chinese employees' own perceptions of work conflict.

Perception often appears with 'of' alongside 'attitudes', 'success', 'failure', and 'risk'.

Their perception of success might be completely different from the entrepreneurs'.

A number of adjectives can modify perception, including 'general', 'widespread', 'accurate', and 'clear'.

There is a general perception that these products have been poorly marketed.

Usage notes: The adjectives can be distinguished. 'Perceptive' means someone having good insight or understanding (*They were very perceptive to these cues*). 'Perceptible' means something is able to be seen, heard, or noticed (*The objects were only perceptible to those in the front row*).

Second check

A Which of the ten key terms do these synonyms relate to?

to skip, exclude   _____

view, opinion   _____

irony, puzzle   _____

compensate, balance _____

B Replace the struck-through word(s) with a word from the ten available.

We looked at the ~~idea~~ _____ of unique achievement in this field.

There was a ~~little~~ _____ change in the method here.

The article was only a brief ~~sketch~~ _____ of the main points.

Shareholders may well ~~not agree~~ _____ to these plans.

C Select an appropriate option to match the key term.

In 2010, she oversee/oversaw/overseen the restructure of the company.

They should have omitted this to/with/from the report.

Montel (2010) also looked at the notion with/of/for naturalization.

15

persistent pervasive plausible portray
precede preclude predominantly
preliminary premise prevalent

First stage: Introducing the terms

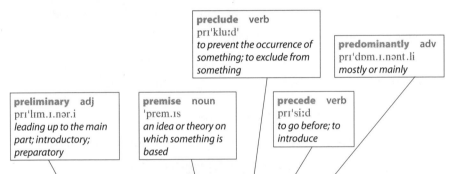

preclude verb
prɪˈkluːd'
to prevent the occurrence of
something; to exclude from
something

predominantly adv
prɪˈdɒm.ɪ.nənt.li
mostly or mainly

preliminary adj
prɪˈlɪm.ɪ.nər.i
leading up to the main
part; introductory;
preparatory

premise noun
ˈprem.ɪs
an idea or theory on
which something is
based

precede verb
prɪˈsiːd
to go before; to
introduce

A **preliminary** review of the building plans **preceded** the visit to the site. Unfortunately, work commitments **precluded** the owner from being available on the day, though the meeting was **predominantly** for the workers and staff. The majority of them rejected the **premise** that the redevelopment was designed to improve the conditions for the employees. The interviews (see Chapter 6) also revealed that the **persistent** misuse of funds on projects such as this was a **prevalent** issue. One worker said that the improvement being based on industry standards was **plausible** but that dishonesty was **pervasive** in the company—a sentiment **portrayed** by the body language of several other members of staff.

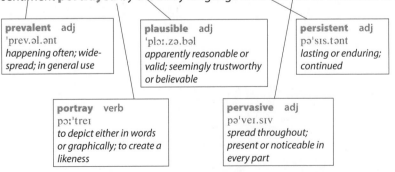

prevalent adj
ˈprev.əl.ənt
happening often; wide-
spread; in general use

plausible adj
ˈplɔː.zə.bəl
apparently reasonable or
valid; seemingly trustworthy
or believable

persistent adj
pəˈsɪs.tənt
lasting or enduring;
continued

portray verb
pɔːˈtreɪ
to depict either in words
or graphically; to create a
likeness

pervasive adj
pəˈveɪ.sɪv
spread throughout;
present or noticeable in
every part

First check

A Circle the adjectives in this list.

preliminary   persistent   plausible   preclude   premise

B Select a word from the ten key terms to match each definition.

possible   _____

to show   _____

noticeable throughout   _____

mainly   _____

C Underline the terms that are misspelled in this extract.

Poverty is prevelent in the country but occurs predominantely in the rural areas. Manning (1978) portrayed a country living in fear of the despots in power and their persistent attempts to destabilize the rural south. The theory was plausible at the time, but after numerous regime changes the preliminary Western-backed government is working hard to reduce this pevasive economic hardship through locally run initiatives.

Second stage: Collocations and usage

Persistent is an adjective that can be used directly before a noun to modify it (*persistent gap*) or after a linking verb (*had become persistent*). It has a related adverb form, **persistently**, and a related noun form, **persistence**.

> **Better than** constant, lasting

Groups at risk of persistent poverty are mainly children and large rural families.

Persistent is often used with 'nature', 'myth', 'approach', 'gap', 'difficulties', 'problems', and 'pain'.

The persistent problems faced by the trust led to its closure in 2005.

It signified Bush Sr.'s persistent approach towards maintaining cordial ties with China.

Usage notes: Persistent implies continued action but has the specific meaning of enduring and relentless if the agent is an action or event (*persistent losses*) or stubbornly if the agent is a person (*persistent attempts*). It often has a negative connotation.

Nearly three-quarters of those surveyed labelled their pain as persistent.

Pervasive   is an adjective that can be used directly before a noun to modify it (*pervasive nature*) or after a linking verb (*appear pervasive*). It has a related adverb form, pervasively, and a related noun form, pervasiveness.

Better than widespread, everywhere

Engagement is a pervasive procedure which cannot focus on any particular person, incident, or behaviour.

Things can have a pervasive 'nature', 'influence', or 'effect'.

For several years, it had a pervasive effect on their design thinking.

They highlighted the pervasive influence of Italian-American gangster films.

Usage notes: Pervasive tends to be a judgement and often expresses negative things. It is used to describe something that has spread throughout. The comparable term 'prevalent' means widespread due to something that has prevailed, perhaps having beaten off competition, or that is in general use. Prevalent can also mean predominant (*The most prevalent cause is lack of concentration*).

Plausible   is an adjective that can be used directly before a noun to modify it (*plausible reason*) or after a linking verb (*This is plausible*). It has a related adverb form, plausibly.

Better than possible, likely, believable

Although at first this tool seemed plausible, further evaluation showed that its explanatory power was severely restricted.

'Arguments', 'explanations', 'conclusions', and 'reasons' can all be plausible.

The only plausible explanation is that the component was not fastened properly.

The literature has yet to provide a plausible reason for this result.

Usage notes: As seen above, 'plausible' tends to relate to an explanation, argument, or statement. It implies that something sounds logical and may be true. 'Possible' tends to relate to events and the likelihood that an event will happen.

The reason they gave was plausible.

It is still possible that the meeting will take place before the end of the month.

Portray is a regular verb. Its past participle is portrayed and present participle is portraying. It has a related noun form, portrayal.

Better than show, reveal

Qualitative approaches seek to portray a world in which reality is socially constructed and ever-changing.

Portray is often preceded by 'seek to', 'attempt to', and 'tend to'.

We have attempted to portray the feelings of the employees regarding these changes.

It is commonly followed by 'as'.

These native actors are often portrayed as villains on screen.

Precede is a regular verb. Its past participle is preceded and present participle is preceding.

Better than come first, go before, lead

This translation by Rossetti precedes all of the above works.

Precede often takes the adverbs 'directly', 'immediately', and 'typically'.

These must be capitalized when they directly precede an individual's name.

Sustainability typically precedes preservation in this situation.

Usage notes: Precede is often confused with the verb 'proceed', which means to begin something or to carry on. As an example of its definition of place and position, it is employed to express that a work or study came before another (as in the first example above) or someone came before someone else in a particular field or role.

Her older sister, who took on the role in 1823, was preceded by the psychologist Richard Gunther.

Preclude   is a regular verb. Its past participle is **precluded** and present participle is **precluding**.

Better than prevent, stop

Kezar (2010) suggests that these policies will definitely preclude some poor students from entering the institutions.

Preclude is often followed by the noun phrases 'the use' and 'the need'.

This is unlikely to preclude the need for more spending on advertising.

The preposition 'from' is often used with preclude.

It also automatically precludes an area from being designated as historic.

Usage notes: Preclude is similar in meaning to 'prevent' but tends to be used only in scenarios where something has been 'ruled out' because of something else. Prevent has a broader meaning and is especially used when someone has stopped something from happening or taken a measure to avert it.

Having a parent or grandparent with the condition precludes them from taking part.

This drink should also prevent them from being dehydrated during the test.

Predominantly   is an adverb that tends to come before the term it is modifying. It has a related adjective form, **predominant**.

Better than mainly, largely, mostly

Boards predominantly comprise individuals with similar gender, age, background, and experience.

Usage notes: Predominantly is a synonym of primarily, and both these adverbs mean mainly (to a large degree/usually). When the meaning relates to mostly (in most cases/greatest number), then predominantly is preferred.

This is primarily a review article on the cases that have been reported so far.

This tree is predominantly seen in the north of the country.

Preliminary

Preliminary is an adjective that is mainly used directly before a noun to modify it (*preliminary findings*). It has a related noun form, **preliminary**.

> **Better than** first, opening

The time between the preliminary tests and the main tests was short.

Preliminary often modifies the nouns 'investigation', 'findings', 'questions', and 'evaluation'.

For this reason it is useful to ask a few preliminary questions.

A topic of this size will require some preliminary investigation.

Premise

Premise is a countable noun. It has a related verb form, **premise**.

> **Better than** basis, idea

An empirical study of the US-China bilateral economic relations was conducted under these premises.

Things can be 'built on' or 'based on' a premise.

This theory was built on the premise that employees in this role are not seeking advancement in the workplace.

Often, premise is preceded by 'accept', 'support', or 'reject'.

We reject the premise that these groups are the only ones that can be termed 'endemic'.

Usage notes: There is another plural noun (occurring only in the plural) with the same spelling that means a piece of land on which a business or house is located (*the company's premises*). It is unrelated to this entry.

Prevalent

Prevalent is an adjective that can be used directly before a noun to modify it (*prevalent measure*) or after a linking verb (*tends to be prevalent*). It has a related noun form, **prevalence**.

> **Better than** widespread, common

Celebrity endorsement is an increasing trend and a prevalent strategy in many business practices.

Prevalent is normally graded with the terms 'most' / 'least' or 'more' / 'less'.

Since the industry is expected to perform well in the next few years, such behaviour will become more prevalent.

It can be used with the prepositions 'among' and 'in' / 'within'.

Domestic abuse is prevalent in society, as the statistics below demonstrate.

Usage notes: Prevalent means widespread due to something that has prevailed, perhaps having beaten off competition, or that is in general use. Prevalent can also mean predominant (*The most prevalent cause is lack of concentration*).

Pervasive tends to be a judgement and often expresses negative things. It is used to describe something that has spread throughout (see separate entry above).

📋 Second check

A Which of the ten key terms do these synonyms relate to?

widespread, everywhere   _____

to show, reveal   _____

possible, likely   _____

to rule out, stop   _____

B Replace the struck-through word with a word from the ten available.

One of the symptoms is a *constant* _____ cough.

The basic *idea* _____ was to give students from low-income families an opportunity to study in the region.

It *mainly* _____ occurs when inflation is low.

Their claims are *possible* _____ but will require further investigation.

C Select an appropriate option to match the key term.

The condition is prevalent at/within/with rural societies.

This will preclude them from/in/to taking part any further.

They are always portrayed between/with/as lazy and ignorant.

16

First stage: Introducing the terms

prominent adj
'prɒm.ɪ.nənt
*well known or important;
standing out or noticeable*

proximity noun
prɒkˈsɪm.ə.ti
*nearness or closeness in time,
distance, or occurrence*

prone adj
prəʊn
*having a tendency to
something; lying face
downwards*

problematic adj
ˌprɒb.ləˈmæt.ɪk
*full of difficulties; likely
to cause problems;
questionable*

prospective adj
prəˈspek.tɪv
*of or in the future;
anticipated or likely*

There has been support for the notion that a **prospective** board member who is related to a current member might lead to a **problematic** situation. This **proximity** means that new members could be **prone** to voting the same way as their **prominent** relations. Yang (2015) **recalls** a situation where a young member who had gained **recognition** for his innovation and who was a **proponent** of the 'Vision Principle' lost a key vote, **primarily** due to the senior board members garnering support from their cousins and nephews to oppose the motion. Chanchenkit (2013) and Kaotira (2007) have **probed** comparable cases occurring in Thailand.

recognition noun
ˌrek.əgˈnɪʃ.ən
*acknowledgement
or identification of
something; agreement
that something is true*

recall verb
rɪˈkɔːl
*to remember or
recollect; to call back
or ask to return*

proponent noun
prəˈpəʊ.nənt
*a person who puts forward
something; a person who
supports something*

primarily adv
praɪˈmer.əl.i
*mainly; chiefly;
originally*

probe verb
prəʊb
*to examine thoroughly;
to question indirectly*

✐ First check

A   Circle the nouns in this list.

probe   prominent   proponent   recall   recognition

B   Select a word from the ten key terms to match each definition.

having a tendency to do   _____

chiefly   _____

noticeable   _____

to recollect   _____

C   Underline the terms that are misspelled in this extract.

The proximity of the object is the reason for the high recogntion scores. The leading scores were achieved primarily by groups two and three. Group one was prone to forget these objects and, in fact, recalling even half proved problematic for many of them.

Second stage: Collocations and usage

Primarily   is an adverb that can be used as a sentence adverb (see 24) at the start of a sentence. It can be used before or after the word it is modifying.

> **Better than** mainly, largely

The strategy, however, was based primarily on the assumption that school fees were the main obstacle to universal primary education.

Primarily is usually paired with the participles 'used', 'based', 'influenced', or 'interested'.

The clothing brand is influenced primarily by skateboarding.

primarily, probe, problematic, prominent, prone,
proponent, prospective, proximity, recall, recognition
119

Usage notes: Primarily is a synonym of predominantly (see 15), and both these adverbs mean mainly (to a large degree/usually). When the meaning relates to mostly (in most cases/greatest number), then predominantly is preferred.

This is primarily a review article on the cases that have been reported so far.

This is predominantly seen in the north of the country.

Probe is a regular verb. Its past participle is probed and present participle is probing.

Better than search, look, research, enquire into

I found this the best way to probe the life stories of these three subjects.

The preposition 'for' can be used after probe.

Interviewers must probe for more information during this phase.

Usage notes: Often probe is used in relation to questions or responses. Especially common is to ask 'probing questions'.

This was a training activity to teach interviewers the skill of asking probing questions.

These follow-up questions are designed to probe their initial responses and extract further data.

Problematic is an adjective that can be used directly before a noun to modify it (*problematic situation*) or after a linking verb (*can become problematic*). It has another form, problematical.

Better than tricky, difficult

Reforms that caused a conflict of interest were even more problematic for these parties.

Things tend to 'become', 'remain', or 'prove' problematic.

It only becomes problematic with the addition of a third layer.

Things are 'often', 'particularly', or 'deeply' problematic.

This transition into the workplace can often be problematic.

In larger datasets this issue is particularly problematic.

Prominent   is an adjective that can be used directly before a noun to modify it (*prominent features*) or after a linking verb (*is prominent*). It has a related adverb form, **prominently**.

> **Better than** noticeable, obvious

Cosmetic facial procedures are the most popular surgery type, since the face is perceived as the most prominent and defining physical feature.

Things often 'become' or 'remain' prominent. Nouns associated with prominent include 'figure', 'role', 'factor', and 'example'.

This remains a prominent example of a sustainable business nearly 40 years later.

Prominent takes both the preposition 'in' and the adverb 'as'.

He became a prominent figure in the reform of the state.

This kind of support is no longer as prominent as it was in the 1980s and 1990s.

Usage notes: There is a related noun form, 'prominence', and things or people tend to 'rise to prominence'; but the adjective is more versatile and easier to employ.

Prone   is an adjective that is used after a linking verb (*seem prone to this*). It has a related noun form, **proneness**.

> **Better than** likely (to), usually, at risk (of)

As an 'instrument of data collection' the researcher is prone to bias.

Prone tends to be associated with 'error', 'violence', 'flooding', and 'bias'.

The measures must be taken, as these prisoners are prone to violence.

Prone is used alongside the preposition 'to' and often takes the adverbs 'highly', 'particularly', and 'especially'.

These patients are especially prone to hip fracture.

Usage notes: Prone only comes before a noun to modify it when the meaning of 'lying downwards' is intended.

The prone patients were then asked to slowly sit up and take a sip of water.

Proponent   is a countable noun.

Better than follower, fan, supporter

The majority of researchers concentrate on the interactions between proponents and opponents of these new practices.

Proponent is often used with the adjectives 'strong', 'avid', 'true', 'leading', and 'long-time'. The preposition 'of' follows it.

She was a leading proponent of pacifism in the country.

Usage notes: Proponent can be used for political purposes such as for supporting 'democracy', 'rights', 'peace', and for systems, methods, and theories.

Most were proponents of heliocentrism.

Prospective   is an adjective that is used directly before a noun to modify it (*prospective client*). It has a related adverb form, prospectively.

Better than likely, future, probable

Experience is recognized as a key attribute that employers look for in a prospective employee.

Prospective normally modifies nouns such as 'study', 'students', 'teachers', 'clients', 'outcomes', and 'cohort'.

The policy only applied to prospective students and those on distance learning courses.

The different retrospective and prospective outcomes from these studies will be outlined next.

Usage notes: Care should be taken so as not to confuse this adjective with the noun 'perspective'.

Proximity   is an uncountable noun.

Better than closeness, nearness

Territories adjacent, or in proximity, were also included in the scheme.

Proximity is normally used in the form 'in proximity to', 'proximity to', and 'in the proximity of'.

Proximity to the customer is another key factor that will bring benefits.

This strategy allows the retailer to reach shoppers that are in proximity to the store via the app.

Usage notes: 'Close' is by far the most common adjective that modifies proximity. Because the noun itself means closeness or nearness however, this adjective use is considered redundant.

Recall   is a regular verb. Its past participle is **recalled** and present participle is **recalling**.

> **Better than** remember, as mentioned earlier

This was largely due to the nature of assessment, which mainly required students to recall facts with no higher-order thinking.

Adverbs that are associated with recall include 'clearly', 'distinctly', 'vaguely', and 'suddenly'.

When asked, the manager said he vaguely recalled something like that happening.

Usage notes: Recall is also employed to mean that something has been asked to be returned, such as a product that has been shown to be faulty.

The company recalled 3,000 cars of this model, following concerns over jamming pedals.

The meaning 'to remember or recollect' is quite conversational and best employed when relating what an interviewee has said and to remind the reader of something.

Recall that the employee had no prior experience of using the system.

It is often used in this way in the mathematical sciences.

Recall that this function can be defined as ...

Another meaning is as a synonym of evoke and of reminding someone of something.

The author's last novel actually recalls the spirit of the early work of Duman.

Recognition is an uncountable noun. It has a related verb form, recognize.

Better than credit, realization, remembering

Sales promotion can enhance brand recognition and brand recall, leading to future purchase.

Several verbs are associated with recognition. They include 'gain', 'achieve', 'earn', 'receive', 'deserve', and 'seek'. Recognition is also seen in the phrase 'lack of recognition'.

There has been a lack of recognition of the challenges facing these families.

The prepositions that can be used are 'for', 'as', 'without', and 'by' / 'from'.

The country's leaders sought recognition as a major power through these policies.

Recognition from their peers was another aspiration for these workers.

Usage notes: Recognition represents a desire to be recognized either for an action that has been carried out or for standing and status in a field or industry. It also means accepting that something exists or is important (*There is general recognition that the government can no longer ignore this problem*).

✍ Second check

A Which of the ten key terms do these synonyms relate to?

well known, obvious   _____

to remember, bring to mind   _____

likely to, predisposed   _____

difficult, awkward   _____

B Replace the struck-through word with a word from the ten available.

The *nearness* _____ of the town was an issue that had to be overcome.

This is *mostly* _____ experienced prior to breakfast.

It was of great interest to *supporters* _____ of nutritional profiling.

A number of other areas would need to be *searched* _____ .

C Select an appropriate option to match the key term.

The latter region is also more prone to/for/at earthquakes.

The participants continued to probe with/for/to a solution to the first task.

They were also prominent in/on/of the field of astrophysics.

17

refine reflect reinforce relatively reliance renewed replicate reportedly resolve respective

First stage: Introducing the terms

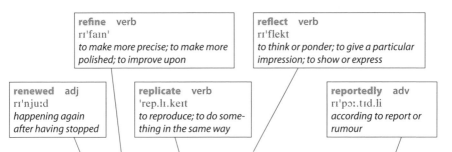

refine verb
rɪˈfaɪn
to make more precise; to make more polished; to improve upon

reflect verb
rɪˈflekt
to think or ponder; to give a particular impression; to show or express

renewed adj
rɪˈnjuːd
happening again after having stopped

replicate verb
ˈrep.lɪ.keɪt
to reproduce; to do something in the same way

reportedly adv
rɪˈpɔː.tɪd.li
according to report or rumour

The next step is to **refine** our study to **reflect** the latest changes to the national policy. The **renewed** focus on education is welcome, with **reportedly** $500 million being made available to **replicate** the success of the central provinces (Quebec and Ontario and their **respective** capitals Quebec City and Toronto). The **resolve** of the central government has been tested by the negativity surrounding many recent policies and their **reliance** on foreign 'czars' to direct their efforts, but the latest move to **reinforce** the premium school scheme with investment has been **relatively** well received.

relatively adv
ˈrel.ə.tɪv.li
in comparison to someone or something else

reliance noun
rɪˈlaɪ.əns
dependence on something or someone; confidence or trust

respective adj
rɪˈspek.tɪv
belonging or relating separately to each of several entities

resolve verb
rɪˈzɒlv
to deal with conclusively; to solve or end a problem

reinforce verb
ˌriː.ɪnˈfɔːs
to make something stronger; to increase; to make more effective

✏️ First check

A   Circle the verbs in this list.

reflect   reliance   replicate   reportedly   respective

B   Select a word from the ten key terms to match each definition.

to copy	_____
to strengthen	_____
to end a problem	_____
based on rumour	_____

C   Underline the terms that are misspelled in this extract.

This has reportedley been done by a number of researchers. Indeed, with the renewed interest in this topic, McClaren and Noades (2003) have refined their guidelines to reflect current practice. We replicate the structure in Figure 9 with the areas they have attempted to resolve and highlight the receptive changes made to the two sets.

Second stage: Collocations and usage

Refine   is a regular verb. Its past participle is **refined** and present participle is **refining**. It has a related noun form, **refinement**.

> **Better than** make better, improve

Caughey (1994) states that young admirers want to refine their personality traits to be similar to those of their idols.

'Skills', 'understanding', 'meaning', 'questions', 'designs', and 'models' tend to be refined.

The pilot study was to give initial feedback to help refine the questions for the actual questionnaire study.

Three weeks have been allocated to refine the designs before they are resubmitted.

Usage notes: Refine implies that the level or quality of something is being raised (improved) rather than just a change or modification occurring. We use refine when small changes are required—often because of feedback, a change of circumstances, or a less than perfect outcome.

Reflect is a regular verb. Its past participle is reflected and present participle is reflecting. It has a related adjective form, reflective, and noun reflection.

Better than show, indicate, mean, think

This reflects the fact that banks only report a notional amount for these activities.

Reflect often relates to 'opinions' or 'changes'.

The document dated 5th May reflects the changes made following our meeting.

Adverbs that are regularly employed include 'adequately', 'accurately', 'clearly', 'critically', and 'carefully'.

The guide has been produced to instruct writers on how to critically reflect on their work.

This communication ensures that the quality and delivery time of the products adequately reflect the high prices of this region.

Reflect is followed by the prepositions 'on' and 'upon', with little difference in meaning between the two.

The trainees are given a journal so they can reflect on/upon their first week.

Usage notes: Reflect can mean both to think seriously and consider (*We will have to reflect on these findings*) and to show, serve, or give evidence of the characteristics of something (*This success reflects the amount of work that has gone into the project / It reflects well on the school*).

Reinforce is a regular verb. Its past participle is reinforced and present participle is reinforcing. It has a related adjective form, reinforceable, and related noun form, reinforcement.

Better than support, boost, make stronger

This example reinforces the findings of Wetland (2003) and Chew and Chan (2008).

Reinforce tends to be used with 'learning', 'ideas', and 'behaviour'.

The measure is designed to reinforce desired behaviour.

Usage notes: Remember that the prefix 're-' implies 'again', so something must have been carried out initially (*Having further examples will help to reinforce the learning*). Using it in this next example would therefore be incorrect; 'enforce' should be used instead:

Many commentators believe this piece of legislation will be difficult to reinforce.

Relatively
is an adverb that tends to modify adjectives more than it modifies verbs. It has a related adjective form, relative.

Better than more or less, fairly

According to Marl (1988), the process is relatively difficult for newcomers.

The adjectives that are modified by relatively include 'high', 'low', 'short', 'small', 'new', and 'unknown'.

It was a relatively short project, given their previous ventures.

She was relatively unknown in the industry when she took over the company in 1991.

Usage notes: Relatively indicates that the verb it is modifying is being compared with something or someone else. It tends to be used imperfectly as a substitute for 'to a fairly large degree', but then no real comparison is formed.

It was a relatively difficult task to follow. (Relative to what? Have there been previous tasks?)

Here, a comparison has been formed.

Given the circumstances, this is a relatively simple procedure.

This sentence implies that the circumstances are quite challenging or testing, so any procedure would be difficult. But this procedure, although perhaps still difficult, could have been harder than it has turned out to be.

Reliance
is an uncountable noun. It has a related adjective form, reliant.

Better than depending on, support, need

These service brands are vulnerable, due to their heavy reliance on employees with individual traits and personalities.

The adjectives that modify reliance tend to be participles such as 'continued', 'increasing' / 'increased', and 'growing'.

The increasing reliance on imports is also a concern.

The prepositions 'on' and 'upon' are used with reliance. The prefix 'over' is also common.

There is an over-reliance on using these methods for evaluating RPG games.

Renewed   is an adjective that can be used directly before a noun to modify it (*renewed focus*) or after a linking verb (*feel renewed*). It is the past participle of the verb renew. A related adjective form is renewable.

> **Better than** new, changed, restarted

For the US, this was a renewed opportunity for engaging with India, as its foothold in South Asia was limited.

Renewed is often found modifying the nouns 'interest', 'threat', 'focus', 'commitment', and 'optimism'.

Many analysts have forecasted growth and shown renewed optimism in these mergers.

Usage notes: Renewed means to resume something or repeat it but perhaps with more motivation and enthusiasm than before. You can also feel 'renewed', i.e., have more energy and motivation. It also means to merely continue or extend something or to replenish a supply. The latter definition is related to the other adjective, 'renewable', which often comes before 'energy', 'technology', 'source', and 'resource'.

The options for this meaning of replenishment are as follows:

The resource can be renewed.

The resource is renewable.

This is a renewable resource.

Replicate   is a regular verb. Its past participle is replicated and present participle is replicating. It has a related adjective form, replicable.

> **Better than** repeat, copy, redo

The former charity wants to replicate this business model and increase their social impact.

'Findings', 'success', and 'effects' tend to be replicated.

The team was unable to replicate this success in their studies of other rivers in the region.

Usage notes: Replicate may imply something more than just repeat. It is often used when an exact copy or the same result is required (*These cells were then replicated*).

Reportedly
is an adverb that tends to come before the term it is modifying. It can also begin a sentence as a sentence adverb (see 24) (*Reportedly, this measure has yet to be ratified by the authorities*). It has a related adjective form, reported.

Better than apparently, it is believed

The ministry has reportedly spent millions of dollars on schools and given assistance to hundreds of poor families.

Reportedly tends to modify the terms 'offered', 'attracted', 'increased'/'reduced', 'related', and 'associated'.

The use of psychological therapy by practitioners has also reportedly increased.

The company's new owner, DigiPress, also reportedly offered $8.5 million for an existing facility nearby.

Usage notes: Reportedly is used when something has not been proven yet. It is merely what has been 'reported' and is yet to be verified by someone other than the person reporting it. Try to avoid the adverb if something has actually been established or verified. And be mindful of excessive use of adverbs such as 'reportedly', 'allegedly', and 'apparently', as they can make a writer sound lazy and vague and a paper seem under-researched.

Resolve
is a regular verb. Its past participle is resolved and present participle is resolving. It has a related adjective form, resolvable.

Better than solve, settle, work out, answer

This can be applied to resolving problems in the workplace.

Resolve tends to be modified by the adverbs 'fully', 'finally', 'successfully', and 'peacefully'.

When we have conflict, we try to resolve the problems peacefully at the negotiation table.

They successfully resolved the dispute with the suppliers.

The prepositions connected to the verb include 'by' and 'through'.

Most of the cases are resolved through mediation.

Usage notes: This regular verb does not have the meaning of re-solve or solve again. It simply means solve and therefore does not represent repeat action. This is reflected in its pronunciation (rɪˈzɒlv). There is also a noun with the same spelling that means to have determination and purpose (*The members showed a lot of resolve in retaining the original decision*).

Respective   is an adjective that is used directly before a noun to modify it (*respective changes*). It has an adverb form, respectively.

Better than particular, separate, each, individual

This competition is a struggle among different companies to maintain their respective market shares.

Respective is often used with the plural nouns 'fields', 'countries', 'methods', and 'areas'.

The drafters opted for a set of rules based on the respective methods of each party.

Usage notes: The adverb form 'respectively' is found alongside parallel lists to inform the reader that a second list of things is in the same order as a previous list of things. It is used to avoid repetition by not having to write out all the elements again. It is not required if an earlier reference has not been made, such as here. *The weights chosen were 0.2, 0.4, 0.6, and 0.8 respectively.*

An example of the adverb being employed correctly is: '*Meanwhile, the factors B1, B2 and B3 were assessed and produced weights of 0.18, 0.23 and 0.43 respectively.*'

📝 Second check

A Which of the ten key terms do these synonyms relate to?

to hone, improve   _____

to settle, answer   _____

to repeat, copy   _____

trust, dependence   _____

B Replace the struck-through word with a word from the ten available.

They have ~~supposedly~~ _____ seen this species also washing its food before eating it.

This teaching method has been shown to ~~boost~~ _____ learning.

The results ~~display~~ _____ that the process of internal branding is largely influenced by the organization.

~~Dependence~~ _____ on these drugs is well documented.

C Select an appropriate option to match the key term.

Matthews (2001) suggests that the only way to resolve this is │from/through/ in│ hard work.

There is too much reliance │with/in/on│ consultants instead of internal decision making.

Three weeks are allotted for reflecting │to/on/in│ the progress made so far.

18

robust routinely salient signify similarity
situate specialize speculation standing
steadily

First stage: Introducing the terms

speculation noun
spek.jə'leɪ.ʃən
a conclusion reached by basic consideration of a matter

routinely adv
ruː'tiːn.li
regularly; ordinarily

robust adj
rəʊ'bʌst'
strongly built; hardy; effective in most conditions

salient adj
'seɪ.li.ənt
prominent or striking

signify verb
'sɪg.nɪ.faɪ
to be a sign of something; to be of importance or consequence

Speculation is high on whether the team will retain the **salient** features for their latest version. The **robust**-looking outer shell appears to **signify** that safety has been improved, no doubt **routinely** tested at each stage against the previous version. That version had **situated** itself as a recreational vehicle that appealed to the younger buyer. The recent images (Figures 3.4–3.7) also confirm that there is a **similarity** with the rival 5.0, which **specialized** in performance and, after a slow launch, **steadily** improved its **standing** in the field to become one of the outstanding models of the year.

steadily adv
'sted.əl.i
gradually with no real deviation or fluctuation

situate verb
'sɪtʃ.u.eɪt
to put in a particular place; to locate

standing noun
'stæn.dɪŋ
reputation or status; position or rank

similarity noun
ˌsɪm.ɪ'lær.ə.ti
being similar; likeness or resemblance

specialize (BE: specialise) verb
'speʃ.əl.aɪz
to pursue a special line of work or study; to make special or specific; to adapt to certain conditions

✍ First check

A Circle the verbs in this list.

signify   situate   standing   robust   specialize

B Select a word from the ten key terms to match each definition.

to locate   _____

likeness   _____

ordinarily   _____

striking   _____

C Underline the terms that are misspelled in this extract.

A robust clean is routinley carried out by the IT department. Apart from files and databases, any salient problems relating to hardware are logged. As the company specilaises in life insurance, this signifys the need for advanced and frequent security and privacy checks.

Second stage: Collocations and usage

Robust   is an adjective that can be used directly before a noun to modify it (*robust measures*) or after a linking verb (*has to be robust*). It has a related adverb form, **robustly**, and a related noun form, **robustness**.

> **Better than** strong, tough, well investigated

Asia contains some of the world's most robust economies and represents more than 40% of global trade.

There a number of nouns that are modified by robust. They include 'measure', 'policy', 'response', 'evidence', 'approach', 'system', 'effort', and 'feature'.

These rules are very important for a robust system to work effectively.

Tell and Dun (2004) use robust methods to analyse these implications.

Adverbs that modify robust include 'fairly', 'sufficiently', and 'physically'.

It was considered a fairly robust response in the circumstances.

Routinely is an adverb that tends to come before the term it is modifying. It has a related noun and adjective form, routine.

Better than normally, usually

A previously published questionnaire was used to routinely assess the presence of these symptoms.

Routinely tends to be used with 'perform', 'discuss', 'assess', 'occur', and 'manage'.

These security checks are routinely performed.

Most of the fieldwork involved routinely assessing the individual stages of development.

Salient is an adjective that is used directly before a noun to modify it (*salient point*).

Better than main, leading, noticeable

The textbook fails to include salient exercises that can motivate the learners.

Salient is primarily used alongside 'features' and 'point'.

Therefore, a salient feature is that, in the construction of animation settings, a subjective ideology is able to be built.

Usage notes: Salient is used to describe something that stands out or is significant. It does not describe the main feature or most common feature of something. The salient feature of a book might be its illustrations or just one small, but significant, section.

Signify is a regular verb. Its past participle is signified and present participle is signifying. It has a related adjective form, signifiable, and related noun form, signifier.

Better than show, mean

Additionally, these issues signify the complexity of inclusion.

'Importance', 'change', and 'progress' tend to be signified.

Arrows connecting these points signify change within the system.

Similarity   is a noun that can be either countable or uncountable.

Better than likeness, match

Then, its similarity or difference will be reflected in the multicultural policymaking process.

The prepositions to use with similarity are 'between', 'in', 'to', and 'with'.

There is a similarity in the number of formal long-term plans used.

The semantic similarity between these words is a problem for programmers.

Usage notes: The similarity between two things can be quite high, making them almost the same (*striking similarity, remarkable similarity, obvious similarity*); or there can be just a passing resemblance between them (*possible similarity, rough similarity, a degree of similarity*).

Situate   is a regular verb. Its past participle is situated and present participle is situating.

Better than place, position, set

The target learners of the present study are situated between the second (CI) and the third (CC) stages.

'Work' or 'research' tends to be situated.

This is in order to better situate our research within current social science debate.

The reflexive pronouns 'itself' and 'themselves' also often follow situate.

Assessors were able to situate themselves fully within the mainstream community.

Usage notes: Situate is mainly used figuratively in academic writing to give context and placement to something that has been created, discovered, or proposed (*It is interesting that they have situated their work alongside these conventional narratives*). Situate is used less often to express that something has been physically placed somewhere. Place and position work just as well in this instance (*We must take care when considering where to place/position/situate the sculptures*).

Specialize   is a regular verb. Its past participle is specialized and present participle is specializing. It has a related noun form, specialization.

Better than focus, concentrate on

Ms Lee's suggestions are relevant because she specializes in teaching children of this age.

The preposition 'in' is used after specialize.

The group specializes in creating authentic experiences for clients.

Usage notes: When the past participle modifies a noun, the meaning relates to something designed for a specific purpose or use (*specialized equipment, specialized training*). The noun 'specialist' relates to a person and should not be employed as an adjective (NOT *specialist equipment*).

Speculation   is an uncountable and a countable noun. It has a related verb form, speculate.

Better than rumour, opinion, guess

I discovered that my speculations were consistent with those of previous literature.

People can 'engage in' speculation, 'increase' it and 'end' it.

Such growth is likely to increase speculation that the US Federal Reserve will raise interest rates.

Prepositions used with speculation include 'about', 'over', and 'on'.

Speculation over the future of the minister continued to grow; a number of colleagues had already been lined up as possible replacements.

Usage notes: The noun is also found in phrases that are perhaps too informal or journalistic for academic texts (*'speculation was rife', 'speculation was rampant', 'speculation was fuelled'*).

Standing   is an uncountable noun.

Better than position, place

The reforms improved the country's standing in the West.

Standing is often modified by 'equal', 'good', 'low', 'social', and 'public'.

The ministry's public standing was dented when it was revealed they had spent three times their budget.

The two figures involved were of equal standing.

Often standing is 'improved' or 'enhanced'.

This was designed to improve their standing in the 1972 presidential contest.

Steadily   is an adverb that can come before or after the term it is modifying. It has a related adjective form, **steady**.

Better than bit by bit, slowly, solidly

The JFTC steadily increased its influence during the 1990s.

Steadily tends to modify the terms 'grow', 'increase', 'rise', 'fall', 'decline', and 'diminish'.

The minimum recognized level of education has steadily declined.

The management team is also pleased that the client base is steadily growing.

Usage notes: This is a versatile adverb with synonyms that include gradually, evenly, and regularly. That said, it suggests a slightly higher or better performance than 'gradually'. When used for growth, it has a positive and favourable implication. A company with steady growth is doing well.

The company has experienced an upturn in fortunes and grown steadily since entering these new markets.

 **Second check**

A Which of the ten key terms do these synonyms relate to?

show, mean   _____

well developed, strong   _____

increasingly, bit by bit   _____

place, position   _____

B Replace the struck-through word(s) with a word from the ten available.

Each node was ~~often~~ _____ checked for duplicates.

The tutors were concerned about the ~~likeness~~ _____ of the two projects.

These programs have ~~inch by inch~~ _____ improved over the years.

There was some ~~rumour~~ _____ that the project would be delayed, or perhaps even cancelled.

C Select an appropriate option to match the key term.

Cheung (2014) noticed there was a similarity of/for/with Lam's theory.

This prompted speculation of/under/over whether they could sustain this growth.

The case study company specializes from/in/at advising other firms about their CSR activities.

19

subjective subsequently substantial
sufficiently suitability susceptible symbolize
systematic tendency theoretical

First stage: Introducing the terms

> **tendency** noun
> 'ten.dən.si
> *an inclination or likelihood; a natural disposition for something to go a certain way*

> **subjective** adj
> səb'dʒek.tɪv'
> *influenced by personal feelings or beliefs rather than evidence or facts*

> **theoretical** adj
> θɪə'ret.ɪ.kəl
> *existing only in theory not practice; speculative*

> **susceptible** adj
> sə'sep.tə.bəl
> *liable to experience, or be influenced by, something*

> **substantial** adj
> səb'stæn.ʃəl
> *considerable in amount or size; important; sufficient*

The **theoretical** review by Jones (2003) presented a **substantial** body of literature but had the **tendency** to drift into a **subjective** evaluation of each work. Han (2005) is also regarded as being **susceptible** to introducing his own theories into these summaries. The ICS was the first group to study the reviews and award a score based on the **suitability** of the reviewer. They reported that only Wilson (2006) and Deng (2005) **sufficiently** demonstrated a **systematic** and objective analysis of the topic. **Subsequently,** the ICS moved onto portfolios, which perhaps **symbolizes** the group's inability to see studies through to a satisfactory conclusion.

> **suitability** noun
> ˌsuː.tə'bɪl.ə.ti
> *appropriateness; acceptability*

> **sufficiently** adv
> sə'fɪʃ.ənt.li
> *to a suitable or sufficient degree*

> **systematic** adj
> ˌsɪs.tə'mæt.ɪk
> *methodical; arranged in a system; carried out in a step-by-step manner*

> **symbolize** (BE: symbolise) verb
> 'sɪm.bəl.aɪz
> *to stand for or represent; to be a symbol of*

> **subsequently** adv
> sʌb.sɪ.kwənt.li
> *later, afterwards; in the end*

📋 First check

A Circle the adjectives in this list.

substantial   systematic   tendency   theoretical   subjective

B Select a word from the ten key terms to match each definition.

afterwards   _____

step by step   _____

ample   _____

to stand for   _____

C Underline the terms that are misspelled in this extract.

They do not become sufficientley advanced, and this is why systematic reviews have been conducted (Porm 2001, Ren 2004, Sanchez 2005). A substantal number of the organisms are susceptible to the disease. The tendency to live near water and their sutability as a host for the parasite are key factors.

Second stage: Collocations and usage

Subjective is an adjective that can be used directly before a noun to modify it (*subjective view*) or after a linking verb (*will always be subjective*). It has a related adverb form, subjectively, and a related noun form, subjectivity.

> **Better than** personal, individual, biased

The subjective nature of what constitutes entrepreneurial success is an obstacle to this.

Subjective can often be found modifying the nouns 'measure', 'nature', 'judgement', and 'portrayal'.

There is also a growing interest in the objective and subjective portrayal of the phenomenon.

Finally, the reliance on subjective measures is suggested as another factor reducing the credibility of the strategy.

Answers: A substantial, systematic, theoretical, subjective **B** subsequently, systematic, substantial, symbolize **C** sufficiently, suitability, substantial, suitability

Adverbs linked to subjective include 'highly', 'purely', 'largely'.

They were criticized for choosing criteria that were purely subjective.

Usage notes: Subjective has a number of meanings but most relate to personal opinions, feelings, and things formed in the mind rather than happening in the external world. Given that it is fairly difficult not to be subjective when saying something or viewing something, avoid obvious phrases such as 'His opinions were subjective'.

Subsequently   is an adverb that usually comes before the term it is modifying. It is often employed as a sentence adverb (see 24) or a conjunctive at the start of a sentence or a clause respectively. It has a related adjective form, subsequent.

> **Better than** then, after that, later, next

Subsequently, these were given to local businesses and termed donations.

Usage notes: Subsequently means afterwards or after something else has happened. It should not be confused with consequently, which relates to cause and effect, such as something having an impact on or causing something else to happen. Subsequently relates only to order and sequence.

The company had begun life in Hong Kong but subsequently moved to the mainland after a merger in 2000.

In the example above, the move clearly occurred because of the merger, but there is not enough information. This point is not being explicitly made, only the sequence of events, so subsequently is used. In this next example, the cause and effect is clear, so the writer chooses consequently.

The company originated in Hong Kong but merged with a Beijing firm in 2000; consequently, they moved to the mainland where they continued operating for ten years.

Substantial   is an adjective that can be used directly before a noun to modify it (*substantial number*) or after a linking verb (*will prove substantial*). It has a related adverb form, substantially.

> **Better than** sizable, big, large

This was an ambitious report that aimed to make a substantial improvement to the legal certainty of the issue.

subjective, subsequently, substantial, sufficiently, suitability,
susceptible, symbolize, systematic, tendency, theoretical

143

Substantial is used to modify a variety of nouns. Examples include 'increase'/ 'decrease', 'proportion', 'effect', 'improvement', 'interest', and 'threat'.

The Rotterdam Rules have a substantial effect on the allocation of burden of proof.

A substantial increase in the elderly population is expected in the next few decades.

Usage notes: As well as the obvious meanings of a considerable amount, size, or quantity, substantial can mean sufficient or even perhaps too much (*The amount of time they had allocated was substantial, considering the size of the class*).

Sufficiently is an adverb that can come before or after the term it is modifying. It has a related adjective form, **sufficient.**

Better than enough, amply

It is also important to be aware of all communication channels and sufficiently utilize them.

Sufficiently often modifies the adjectives 'strong', 'robust', 'broad', and 'challenging'.

The literature should be of sufficient originality, and topics should be sufficiently broad.

Suitability is an uncountable noun. It has a related adjective form, **suitable,** and a related adverb form, **suitably.**

Better than correctness, good fit

This is based on the researcher's judgement about the respondent's suitability for the study.

Suitability is used with the prepositions 'of', 'for', and 'to'.

We need to determine the suitability of these devices.

They tested the IT system's suitability for workers who had little computer experience.

Its suitability to the needs of the ESL students was also evident.

Usage notes: In most dictionaries, the nouns suitability and suitableness have the same definition. Given this, the preferred option would be 'suitability', not least because the latter sounds clumsy and awkward. In fact, some vocabulary databases do not even recognize 'suitableness'.

Susceptible   is an adjective that can be used directly before a noun to modify it (*susceptible types*) or after a linking verb (*appear susceptible*). It has a related noun form, susceptibility.

Better than at risk, vulnerable

It proved to be a volatile series that was susceptible to structural changes.

Susceptible is usually modified by 'particularly' and 'highly' and is followed by the preposition 'to'.

Children might be particularly susceptible to these types of injury.

Usage notes: Often, susceptible is describing influence, disease, damage, injury, or bias; therefore, it tends to have a negative connotation and be used as a warning.

Symbolize   is a regular verb. Its past participle is symbolized and present participle is symbolizing. It has a related noun form, symbolization.

Better than show, mean, suggest

Fatherhood symbolizes power, authority, protection, and experience.

Symbolize is often used with the terms 'meant to' and 'come to'.

The mascot has come to symbolize the determination within the club.

Systematic   is an adjective that can be used directly before a noun to modify it (*systematic use*) or after a linking verb (*should be systematic*). It has a related adverb form, systematically.

Better than regular, organized

This factor considers the systematic effects on debt maturity choice.

Systematic tends to modify the nouns 'review', 'use', and 'approach'.

A systematic review of the extant literature then follows.

They had a systematic approach to planning these projects.

Usage notes: Because systematic stands for something that is carried out according to a system or step by step, it can be employed for most things that have been done carefully, efficiently, and thoroughly.

The inspectors were keen to carry out a systematic assessment of how the school met the students' pastoral needs.

subjective, subsequently, substantial, sufficiently, suitability,
susceptible, symbolize, systematic, tendency, theoretical
145

Tendency is a countable noun.

Better than likelihood, habit

The general tendency is for these measures to be more powerful during the implementation and monitoring stage.

Tendencies are often 'general', 'basic', 'natural', or 'central'. The prepositions that follow the noun include 'for', 'of', 'among', and 'towards'.

There is a tendency among graduates to assume they will be rewarded with high salaries.

It is an attempt to counter this natural tendency of the brain.

Usage notes: The singular form is more common than the plural, as shown by the examples above. The plural is used mainly in the behavioural sciences (*suicidal tendencies, psychological tendencies, aggressive tendencies, violent tendencies*) and in political science (*ideological tendencies, separatist tendencies, nationalist tendencies*).

Theoretical is an adjective that can be used directly before a noun to modify it (*theoretical perspective*) or after a linking verb (*This is purely theoretical*). It has a related adverb form, **theoretically**.

Better than imaginary, assumed

This type of person has the ability to create theoretical models.

Theoretical often modifies the nouns 'framework', 'model', 'lens', 'perspective', and 'assumption'.

Mixed methods research may also contain a theoretical lens.

The assumptions offered were purely theoretical.

Usage notes: A comparison with the adjective 'hypothetical' would be useful here. Theoretical is based on theories or ideas and problem-solving. It can mean that something is possible in theory but not necessarily in practice. Hypothetical means that something is either based on guesswork and assumptions (see 3) or is an imaginary event or condition that has been created as an example.

This not only affects our theoretical understanding of reality, but it also has some practical consequences.

Next, we assessed the positive responses from the participants to the hypothetical scenarios.

📝 Second check

A Which of the ten key terms do these synonyms relate to?

to represent, mean   _____

at risk, liable   _____

personal, particular   _____

leaning, liking   _____

B Replace the struck-through word(s) with a word from the ten available.

The ~~large~~ _____ body of work she left has been catalogued and interpreted by various researchers.

Our introduction has now been ~~acceptably~~ _____ changed to reflect the reviewer's comments.

They had concerns over the ~~fitness~~ _____ of the design.

The motto ~~stands for~~ _____ the hardship that this family firm has experienced over the years.

C Select an appropriate option to match the key term.

It is also susceptible | to/from/about | wind erosion.

We would also question its suitability | with/to/for | young children.

This was | worked to/meant to/hoped to | symbolize the indigenous species.

20 trait transition underlying undertake undoubtedly unified utilize variance verify viable

First stage: Introducing the terms

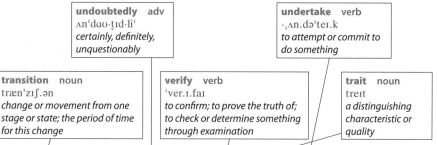

undoubtedly adv
ʌnˈdaʊ·t̬ɪd·li'
*certainly, definitely,
unquestionably*

undertake verb
·ˌʌn.dəˈteɪ.k
*to attempt or commit to
do something*

transition noun
trænˈzɪʃ.ən
*change or movement from one
stage or state; the period of time
for this change*

verify verb
ˈver.ɪ.faɪ
*to confirm; to prove the truth of;
to check or determine something
through examination*

trait noun
treɪt
*a distinguishing
characteristic or
quality*

Effective leaders **undoubtedly** have similar **traits**, allowing them to make the **transition** from being a general worker to **undertaking** managerial duties. This lack of **variance** between the subjects **verified** Lam's theory, as it revealed that there is an **underlying** determination and resolve in all managers. We view this theory as the most **viable** for our study and therefore will **utilize** it to pursue our aim of developing a **unified** theory of leadership style.

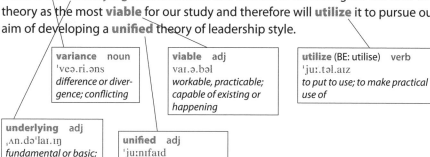

variance noun
ˈveə.ri.əns
*difference or diver-
gence; conflicting*

viable adj
vaɪ.ə.bəl
*workable, practicable;
capable of existing or
happening*

utilize (BE: utilise) verb
ˈjuː.təl.aɪz
*to put to use; to make practical
use of*

underlying adj
ˌʌn.dəˈlaɪ.ɪŋ
*fundamental or basic;
implicit; hidden but
detectable*

unified adj
ˈjuːnɪfaɪd
*formed into a whole;
made into one*

📋 First check

A   Circle the nouns in this list.

utilize   verify   viable   trait   variance

B   Select a word from the ten key terms to match each definition.

to determine something   _____

to make use of   _____

definitely   _____

made into one   _____

C   Underline the terms that are misspelled in this extract.

The transition from three different schemes to a unifed scheme is likely to take some time. Undoubtebly, training will have to be undertaken for those employees who either utilse the booking system or verify the client details.

Second stage: Collocations and usage

Trait   is a countable noun.

> **Better than** feature, manner

A company should execute a tactic that makes use of the traits of the firm.

Trait is often used in conjunction with the following verbs: 'share', 'lack', 'possess', 'acquire', 'develop', 'identify', and 'recognize'.

The system identified traits that were suitable for the role.

It was a trait I recognized in all of the participants.

Trait is also modified by the following adjectives: 'distinctive', 'negative', 'necessary', and 'dominant'.

Luxury brands are afraid of brand demise and losing their necessary traits, that of 'exclusivity' and 'uniqueness'.

Usage notes: A trait tends to be inherited or passed down in people, whereas character is generally said to be influenced by association and the environment. Traits can apply equally to objects and entities as they can to people, as demonstrated in the first and final examples above.

Transition   is a countable and an uncountable noun. It has a related verb form, transition.

Better than change, move, shift

They demonstrated this transition to a more business-minded model.

Something or someone tends to 'make', 'complete', or 'undergo' a transition.

The next stage is for them to make the difficult transition from adolescent to adult.

Adjectives that can modify transition include 'sudden', 'gradual', 'phased', 'smooth', and 'direct'.

Some are now criticizing the fact there is this sudden transition to mixed-ability teaching.

Transition takes the following prepositions: 'in', 'into', 'from', and 'to'.

The transition into or out of special education is one such example.

Usage notes: The verb form has the same meaning as the noun but is less common (. . . *as they transition into adulthood.*)

Underlying   is an adjective that can be used directly before a noun to modify it (*underlying reasons*) or with a linking verb (*remain underlying*). It is the present participle of the verb underlie.

Better than main, basic, causing

The underlying causes of employee behaviour will be investigated according to service performance.

Underlying tends to modify the nouns 'cause', 'condition', 'issue', 'message', 'motive', and 'risk'.

This type of research aims to uncover the underlying motives and desires.

This activity had the underlying message of staying in control and on top of things.

Usage notes: Underlying should not be split into two parts (*'under lying these systems'*). The verb 'underlie' from which the adjective derives (as its present participle) is an irregular verb, the simple past form being 'underlay' and the past participle 'underlain'.

Undertake is an irregular verb. Its past participle is undertaken and present participle is undertaking.

Better than carry out, start, take on

A pilot study was undertaken to ensure that the themes were adequate for the research.

Often a person or organization undertakes 'training', 'assessment', 'fieldwork', 'a review' or 'a journey'.

The worker will undertake training and then assessment to determine suitability for the senior level.

Usage notes: Sometimes 'do' and 'did' can sound inelegant (*We did research / They did fieldwork*). Opt for alternatives such as 'carry out', 'conduct', and 'undertake' instead. Usually the verb is used passively as in the first example (*was undertaken*) and is slightly less flexible than the phrasal 'carry out'. Note also the form of the simple past tense, 'undertook'.

Undoubtedly is an adverb that tends to come before the term it is modifying. It can also be employed as a sentence adverb (see 24) at the start of a sentence (*Undoubtedly, this has proven difficult for most participants*).

Better than indeed, definitely, absolutely

Tourism has undoubtedly played a significant role in Australia's economy.

Undoubtedly tends to modify the verbs 'require', 'exist', 'alter', and 'affect'.

The officers will undoubtedly require further information once they have reached the location.

Usage notes: This adverb should be used sparingly, as it is prone to overuse. 'Clearly' and certainly' are useful alternatives. Because undoubtedly is an emphatic term, hedging (modal) terms such as 'might' or 'could' are inappropriate.

Undoubtedly, this might lead to ...   *Undoubtedly, this will lead to* ...

Unified
is an adjective that can be used directly before a noun to modify it (*unified system*) or after a linking verb (*become unified*). It is the past participle of the verb **unify**. A related noun form is **unifier**.

> **Better than** joined, combined

They introduced a unified approach by combining stock and flow.

Unified often modifies the nouns 'model', 'theory', 'system', 'view', 'form', and 'message'.

There is no unified theory of all the fundamental forces recognized by physics.

Utilize
is a regular verb. Its past participle is **utilized** and present participle is **utilizing**. It has a related noun form, **utilization**.

> **Better than** use, make the most of

It rests on the policymaker's ability to fully utilize the research findings.

Utilize tends to be used with the nouns 'system', 'method', 'technology', 'data', 'strengths', and 'ability'.

Distance learning courses in the department utilize this technology the most.

They are not able to utilize their strengths under these conditions.

It is modified by the adverbs 'effectively' and 'fully'.

The next question related to whether they could fully utilize this system.

Usage notes: Utilize can act as a direct substitute for 'use' and is a good choice for scientific writing to get across the point of making the most of a situation. Other times it can sound as though the writer is trying too hard to be academic (*The participants were allowed to utilize a pen for the second task*). 'Use' is perfectly acceptable in most situations, especially commonplace ones.

Variance
is a countable and an uncountable noun.

> **Better than** difference, change, disagreement

This efficient international portfolio should minimize variance for a given rate of return.

Variance tends to be 'explained', 'measured', and 'accounted for'.

This accounted for around 15% of the variance in the accuracy factor.

Usage notes: The phrase 'at variance with' can also be used to mean opposing or in disagreement with (*These hasty conclusions were at variance with their usual cautious approach*).

Verify   is a regular verb. Its past participle is verified and present participle is verifying. It has related noun forms, verification and verifier, and a related adjective form, verifiable.

Better than prove, show

In their investigation, they were able to verify that innovation has a considerable influence on growth.

Verify is often used with the nouns 'data', 'information', 'findings', 'report', and 'accuracy'.

Relevant published documents will be used to crosscheck the information and verify the data.

Three sets were sent to the corresponding participants to verify the accuracy of the transcription.

Usage notes: 'Verify' implies that an investigation needs to be carried out to find the truth or to show that something is correct. 'Confirm' is normally employed when something just needs acknowledgment and when the fact has been largely established.

We just need the teacher to confirm this is true.

Viable   is an adjective that can be used directly before a noun to modify it (*viable measure*) or after a linking verb (*prove viable*). It has a related noun form, viability, and a related adverb form, viably.

Better than able to do, workable, possible

They were concerned that this strategy might not be viable in larger classes.

Viable is often used with the terms 'prove', 'remain', and 'no longer'.

The strategy of keeping China disengaged from Russia was no longer viable.

Adverbs used with the adjective include 'commercially', 'economically', and 'financially'.

Their policies were now motivated by political or sociological reasons rather than by the desire to form economically viable partnerships as in previous years.

Usage notes: Viable and feasible (see 10) are similar in meaning, but a distinction can be made. Feasible is looking at whether something can be carried out, and viable relates to whether something can be successful or sustainable. Doing something might be feasible, but it may not be viable.

Working with these small businesses for longer than a few weeks is not a viable option for the company.

Within this timeframe, the project is not feasible in its current form.

Second check

A Which of the ten key terms do these synonyms relate to?

feature, quality   _____

to use, apply   _____

change, difference   _____

a move, a switch   _____

B Replace the struck-through word with a word from the ten available.

We are interested in the principles ~~causing~~ _____ this social movement.

Fortunately, they were able to make the ~~change~~ _____ from supporting individual clients to dealing with all of the corporate accounts.

Project B is a ~~possible~~ _____ alternative if the backers pull out of Project A.

The plan is to ~~do~~ _____ this testing in April.

C Select an appropriate option to match the key term.

This largely accounts to/from/for the variance seen in Figure 4.23.

The transition with/to/in an intermediate player is complex.

Is this really the most financially/finance/financial viable option?

Final Check for the Top 200

Replace the word in grey with one from the top 200 (see the hints at the end for a possible solution to each one).

It is now important to sketch _____ (A) the method by which the second observation will be carried out. To boost _____ (B) our understanding of the processes involved, we at the start _____ (C) gave _____ (D) fifteen minutes for the practical task and then ten minutes for the participants to have a think _____ (E) on the solutions that came out _____ (F). Three additional staff members were employed to help _____ (G) the shift _____ (H) from practice to reflection—as this proved tricky _____ (I) during the first observation. All of them being the same _____ (J) was considered important when structuring the observation reports; to get _____ (K) a uniform arrangement, the facilitators worked on the documents all as one _____ (L) the following day. The more _____(M) number of observations as the tasks progressed was in stark contrast to the small _____ (N) findings that arose from the pilot study.

The habit _____ (O) for the groups to dismiss the reflection stage as needless ended _____ (P) in weak scores in the first test and bore likeness _____ (Q) with the study and the findings of Chang (2015). Chang is currently working towards getting _____ (R) an understanding of reflective learning; his research for the most part _____ (S) involves trying to see _____ (T) the direction that reflective study takes when carried out in groups.

Hints

A) See Chapter 14	H) See Chapter 20	O) See Chapter 19
B) See Chapter 9	I) See Chapter 16	P) See Chapter 6
C) See Chapter 12	J) See Chapter 5	Q) See Chapter 18
D) See Chapter 2	K) See Chapter 1	R) See Chapter 3
E) See Chapter 17	L) See Chapter 4	S) See Chapter 15
F) See Chapter 8	M) See Chapter 11	T) See Chapter 7
G) See Chapter 10	N) See Chapter 13	

Possible answers

It is now important to outline the method by which the second observation will be carried out. To enhance our understanding of the processes involved, we initially allocated fifteen minutes for the practical task and then ten minutes for the participants to reflect on the solutions that emerged. Three additional staff members were employed to facilitate the transition from practice to reflection—as this proved problematic during the first observation. Consistency was considered important when structuring the observation reports; to accomplish a uniform arrangement, the facilitators worked on the documents collectively the following day. The growing number of observations as the tasks progressed was in stark contrast to the minimal findings that arose from the pilot study.

The tendency for the groups to dismiss the reflection stage as needless culminated in weak scores in the first test and bore similarity with the study and the findings of Chang (2015). Chang is currently working towards attaining an understanding of reflective learning; his research predominantly involves trying to discern the direction that reflective study takes when carried out in groups.

PART B

Academic Word Categories

Words that will prove useful for creating effective academic English are presented in this second part of the book. The terms are grouped by type, meaning, and setting to ensure that they can be easily absorbed and then employed when writing an essay or paper. They are explored through commentaries, semantic lists, definitions, synonyms, collocations or explanations, to differentiate them in the clearest way possible.

21 NOUNS: Action nouns

Although verbs are the obvious choice for expressing action and creating coherent and dynamic writing, concept nouns still feature heavily in academic texts. The particular nouns that follow all relate to action and tend to be employed just as often as their associated verb forms. The emphasis for these first few nouns is on the verbs they form a relationship with.

Nouns of action that are usually 'made'

Researchers and analysts 'make' *projections* about how they see things developing; these will usually be revised at some point. If there is some doubt, or the prediction relates to data or dates, then *approximations* are 'made'. Approximations can also be given and provided, representing *generalizations*. If your predictions are too specific, then *adjustments* (see 1) will be necessary. And if things are not going according to plan, this will lead to *reassessments*, which may be 'required', 'caused' or 'forced'. A *stipulation* is 'made' if you want something included or something addressed. If you are really not happy (usually about someone), you might even 'make' an *accusation*. With *speculation* (see 18) you can 'encourage', 'invite', or 'increase' it, or if necessary 'end' or 'dismiss' it—an action or situation may also 'give rise to' it.

■ EXAMPLES

stipulation: *This was a written stipulation made to cover the issues no longer in dispute.*

accusation: *It began with the student making an accusation about the lack of direct teaching.*

approximation: *The figure is just an approximation we had to give for the initial report.*

More nouns of action

A *consultation* is something you 'have' or you 'hold', often in the health sciences and within the realms of business. *Clarification* can be 'sought', 'called for', or 'required'. You can also 'give' someone or 'provide' someone with clarification if he or she does not quite understand or you have not been clear enough. An *endorsement* is 'given to' something or 'received from' someone. *Reflections* are usually 'about' something or 'on' something, especially on your work, which you 'give' or 'provide' to the reader. These nouns are sometimes used generically, which means that the action is suggested or advised rather than specifically taking place.

■ **EXAMPLES**

endorsement: *An endorsement received from a tutor can also increase their confidence.* (See also 9, 'endorse'.)

clarification: *Questions 3 and 5 required clarification, as there was some confusion with the wording.*

reflection: *Such reflections are simplified into concepts, which in turn serve as the premise for new conclusions.* (See also 17, 'reflect'.)

Nouns that tend to be used in a generic way

The nouns that follow are likely to be used as concepts and therefore likely to have an uncountable sense.

articulation: *This was designed to support the articulation between research and policy process.*

Usage notes: This noun is used for both expressing the importance of communicating effectively (*Articulation of these ideas is necessary from the outset*), and for the shape or manner in which things come together (*The articulation of these groups can take place naturally over time*).

authentication: *The first task is to analyse the authentication procedure that the bank employs.*

Usage notes: Authentication is often found in the field of computer and communication systems and when discussing security. In these scenarios, it refers to establishing whether a person or an action is genuine, as does the verb form 'authenticate'. The verb may also be used when determining whether historical sources are 'authentic' (see 3); for this meaning though, another related noun, 'authenticity', is more likely to be employed than 'authentication'.

categorization: *Most developers would recommend starting with a categorization of the components that are likely to feature.*

Usage notes: Employed less than its associated verb 'to categorize', categorization is normally used when revealing the different stages of a process and the level to which something has been organized (*The level of categorization has also been reduced in this study*). It is used with the prefixes 'de-' and 'mis-' to show a reduction and an error in categorization respectively.

coordination: *The links were built to promote communication and coordination.*

Usage notes: See 6, 'coordinate'.

determination: *The training is designed to test whether they have sufficient determination.*

Usage notes: This noun is mainly used to demonstrate a desire and willingness to do something or see something through (*This determination bodes well for the future*). When used for this purpose it is linked to the adjective 'determined', not the verb 'to determine' (see 7, 'determine'). But it can be used in the same way as the verb for working something out or producing an outcome (*Determination of the width and height must also be included*).

eradication: *Improvement in this area can only take place after the eradication of rural poverty.*

Usage notes: The noun and the associated verb form 'to eradicate' are employed when discussing removing or eliminating detrimental things such as poverty and disease. Avoid using them for when you are simply taking out a feature or a variable from your work and getting rid of mistakes. These terms are too strong for those situations. Opt for 'eliminate' or 'remove' instead.

Eradication of these diseases was the primary objective at this time.

Stage two involved eliminating any errors that had occurred in the first stage.

extraction: *A later chapter will cover the extraction of bacterial DNA.*

Usage notes: This noun is used in the health and biological sciences, geology, engineering, and when removing unwanted data or separating data to see the trends and patterns (*Factor analysis can result in the extraction of one meaningful factor*). It is also commonly used like an adjective to modify another noun (*The extraction method has been taken from Heinz and Deng (1976)*).

formulation: *This is the reason that question formulation is so important when interviewing these learners.*

> **Usage notes:** Although the verb form is commonly employed (see 10, 'formulate'), the noun is used to emphasize the concept or process of creating something by careful planning or thought—usually ideas, principles, laws, and data (*The three focus group sessions led to the formulation of this idea*).

improvisation: *The company built a reputation with their innovation and improvisation.*

> **Usage notes:** As with most noun-verb combinations, the noun 'improvisation' is usually employed generically or conceptually (*The managers also encourage improvisation from their staff during these periods*) and the verb used for an actual instance (*Group 2 improvised on this task and achieved the highest score*).

internalization: *This study investigates the internalization of three types of motivation.*

> **Usage notes:** Primarily used in psychology for the learning of values and attitudes, internalization is preferred to the verb 'to internalize' when emphasizing the concept rather than a specific act.

visualization: *Animation plays an important role in story visualization.*

> **Usage notes:** The noun is commonly found in texts relating to motivational studies and therapy, often modifying another noun (*The visualization techniques proved quite effective*). The verb 'to visualize' has a broader function and can be employed in many areas of study (*Morgan (1963) visualized a smaller product that targeted a wider population*).

People nouns

This next unofficial category of nouns is often overlooked, but the terms appear quite frequently in academic writing. These nouns either state the role that someone has in an official capacity or plays in a certain scenario, or they label a person based on his or her general worldview or stance on a particular subject. Most of them have verb and/or adjective forms.

Nouns that indicate someone's view or specific belief in something

Supporting or following a particular system or a particular cause means you are an *adherent* of it. Arguing in favour, being the first person to do it, and proposing something are the actions of a *proponent*. An *exponent* tends to explain or use an already accepted idea or emphasize something. *Advocates* publically support or recommend a system or method.

■ **EXAMPLES**

adherent: *Adherents of the previous system welcomed the news.*

proponent: *As a proponent of Kant's federalism, they deemed the EU as still preserving the sovereignty of its states.* (See also 16 'proponent'.)

exponent: *He was an early exponent of the technique and was responsible for its subsequent popularity.*

advocate: *Many of the respondents were advocates of government intervention.* (See also 1, 'advocate'.)

Nouns that indicate someone's rejection of or opposition to something

Opponents of particular theories or schemes are *dissenters* if they oppose the standard beliefs or common societal ideas; they are *skeptics* if they simply doubt or question the normal way. *Detractors* criticize someone, often in an unfair or unconstructive manner.

■ **EXAMPLES**

dissenter: *At the time, dissenters would have been punished for their views.*

skeptic: *There were a number of skeptics who doubted whether this could be achieved in the timeframe available.*

detractor: *Despite having his detractors, the manager implemented these changes single-handedly and with little subsequent impact on operations.*

Nouns that state someone's temperament or general beliefs

(an) empiricist: *This is where the empiricists differ from the realists discussed in Chapter 3.*

> **Definition:** someone who believes that experience is the only source of knowledge.
>
> **Usage notes:** The word has an identical adjective form (*The section begins with an introduction to the empiricist method*).

(an) introvert: *Clearly, it was the work of an introvert who had explored these latent meanings.*

Definition: someone who relates to and is concerned with thoughts and feelings rather than social situations; inwardly involved rather than outwardly expressive

(a) moderate: *It was actually a moderate, Kim Hunt, who appealed for parliament to reform.*

Definition: someone who holds balanced and reserved views and is opposed to any extreme thinking

Usage notes: The noun is pronounced the same as the adjective but differently from the verb 'to moderate'.

noun and adjective, ˈmɒd.ər.ət; verb, ˈmɒd.ər.eɪt

(a) pragmatist: *Much of the success can be attributed to the minister being a pragmatist who understood this balance.*

Definition: someone who takes a practical approach to problems and can adapt to situations in order to be successful

Usage notes: A pragmatist will show pragmatism (noun) and be pragmatic (adjective) in approach and behaviour.

(a) rationalist: *Well-known author and rationalist Ravi Singh is the subject of their second article.*

Definition: someone who is concerned with facts that are observable; relying on reason rather than intuition

Usage notes: The identical adjective is commonly used (*Rationalist theories of organization are prominent in the text*).

(a) visionary: *It required the mind of a visionary for the industry to progress.*

Definition: someone with keen foresight and who is innovative; occasionally, someone who is idealistic but perhaps unrealistic

Nouns that detail the role that someone has officially or plays in a certain scenario

These first seven nouns are used to label roles played by people in a specific situation or scenario:

adversary: *The best defence is to attack an adversary's information source.*

> **Definition:** an opponent or an enemy

arbiter: *It seemed that the manager was not able to effectively carry out the role of arbiter in these matters.*

> **Definition:** someone empowered to judge something; someone having complete control over an activity or situation

beneficiary: *The sole beneficiary of this policy was the homeowner.*

> **Definition:** someone who receives or gains a benefit from a situation

> **Usage notes:** 'Recipient' can be used here, but the term also relates to being given or receiving something bad or negative. Beneficiary is always positive so is suitable when someone gains from an action.

custodian: *Initially, consent had to be gained from the custodian of the land.*

> **Definition:** someone who takes care of something; a guardian or keeper

intermediary: *In fact, intermediaries facilitate money-laundering practices between banks and non-financial institutions.*

> **Definition:** someone who acts as a negotiator to help resolve differences between two parties (also a 'mediator') or to aid their activities.

interlocutor: *I tried to make it clear to my interlocutor that I was ready to be earnest and receptive to all questions.*

> **Definition:** a conversation partner or someone who asks the questions in a conversation

protagonist: *The protagonist should ideally be sympathetic in this genre to create a connection with the audience.*

> **Definition:** a principal or leading figure (usually in a book or a play/film); a supporter of a cause

> **Usage notes:** The former definition is more common than the latter, where adherent is more likely to be employed. It is unnecessary to write 'main' protagonist.

*   *   *

This next set of nouns is for roles played by people in an organization or during an event, usually in an official capacity.

collaborator: *An example of each was sent for further analysis to our collaborator, Dr L. Yang.*

Definition: someone who works with someone else on a joint project

facilitator: *The English tutor was regarded as a key facilitator for student–teacher reflection.*

Definition: someone who assists to make something easier either in a leading or a supporting role

operative: *Ten years ago the factory had only human operatives, but now they embrace computerized systems.*

Definition: a worker, usually with a particular skill; an industry worker who handles a particular piece of equipment

Usage notes: This definition is primarily British English. North American usage would consider an operative to be a government/private agent.

practitioner: *The questionnaire was distributed to medical practitioners from three of the trusts.*

Definition: someone engaged in a profession or who teaches a technique

subordinate: *In this instance, one of the subordinates would be tasked with contacting the client.*

Definition: Someone who is below another in rank; an assistant

Ten more nouns of interest

Here are ten more effective nouns that have been chosen for their usefulness and the frequency with which they occur in academic writing. Conduct your own research on these by obtaining a definition, locating some examples of usage, and then employing them in your writing!

calibre	niche
countermeasure	outlet
facet	precursor
gravity	resourcefulness
locus	vigour

22 VERBS: Reporting verbs

Verbs that are used to report things will be required throughout an essay. They should certainly feature in a literature review (to report on someone's research), the findings section (to report the comments of interviewees for instance), and in the conclusion (to report on your own research outcomes). This first set of verbs can be employed when making a strong claim about something.

Verbs that report strong and definitive claims

If clear evidence has been found for something or findings have proved significant, then you can formally declare (*proclaim*) or announce them as true (*attest*). You confirm or *substantiate* when you effectively *demonstrate* something that you assumed to be true. If clear evidence is lacking but you are confident in your claim, then *affirm*, *assert*, and *contend* are appropriate.

■ EXAMPLES

attest: *As the teaching assistant will attest, the class failed to quieten down despite repeated warnings.*

contend: *In addition, they contend that globalization is a social construct based on a structure of interdependence.* (See also 5.)

affirm: *He affirmed that the employee was not present on the day of the incident.*

substantiate: *The growing overseas activities of the company after 2005 substantiate the reports that local markets were saturated.*

Verbs that report the way that something has been (or will be) carried out

A number of reporting verbs feature in the Top 200. See align (1), articulate (3), clarify (4), compile (4), derive (7), determine (7), differentiate (7), disclose (7), elaborate (8), encompass (8), elicit (8), entail (9), envision (9), formulate (10), frame (10), gauge (10), generate (10), hypothesize (11), incorporate (11), interpret (12), modify (13), outline (14), portray (15), probe (16), undertake (20), utilize (20), verify (20).

The following can also be employed.

allude(to): *Morgan and Chen (2001) only alluded to this system in their research.*

> **Definition:** to refer indirectly, briefly or casually

ascertain: *They also ascertained the reasons why Wu (2015) disputed this.*

> **Definition:** to find out with certainty; to determine

aspire: *I focused on Chinese TESOL students, a neglected group in the literature, and aspired to learn about their motivations.*

> **Definition:** to hope or desire; to seek ambitiously

assimilate: *The redundant information in the second cue was assimilated with the response to the green light.*

> **Definition:** to compare or liken; to become or cause to become similar; to learn something and understand it thoroughly; to absorb.

authenticate: *They authenticated the system in front of members of the Royal Society in 1792.*

> **Definition:** to establish as valid or genuine

capture: *It can also capture the uncertainty in the estimation results.*

> **Definition:** to represent or record; to succeed in representing something; to acquire.

corroborate: *These figures were corroborated by the Social Enterprise Survey.*

> **Definition:** to confirm or support (usually with evidence)

counteract: *We can counteract this low pressure with well-placed apertures in the rooms.*

> **Definition:** to use contrary action to oppose or neutralize the threat of something

critique: *First, they critiqued the accounts of China's recent reform process.*

> **Definition:** to review or analyse critically

deduce: *Therefore, it can be deduced that the data sources for the poverty in the country are unreliable.*

> **Definition:** to reach a conclusion by reasoning; to infer

delineate: *Tan and Li (2002) delineate five key issues that are relevant to the political context.*

> **Definition:** to trace the outline of; to precisely describe or outline something

delve: *This is useful for correcting misinterpretations and for delving into specific subthemes.*

> **Definition:** to inquire or research deeply

dissect: *In order to dissect the discourse, three different analytical categories will be used.*

> **Definition:** to examine or analyse in detail

distinguish: *Some writers distinguish between Islam as a religion and the political Islam.*

> **Definition:** to perceive or indicate differences; to discriminate

elucidate: *He elucidated that the role was established to limit the powers of the board.*

> **Definition:** to make clear or to clarify

endeavour: *I endeavoured to be an active listener at all times.*

> **Definition:** to attempt earnestly; to undertake something with purpose

expose: *In the article, Mertens exposes these low labour standards.*

> **Definition:** to uncover or reveal; to present

expound: *Yang (2014) expounds all the arguments relating to learning motivation.*

> **Definition:** to explain in detail; to elaborate

forecast: *They forecast that in 2015 around 30% of jobs in the EU will need higher education qualifications (van Vught 2009: 39).*

> **Definition:** to estimate or predict; to calculate

formalize: *In Chapter 4 we will formalize all these expressions as part of the specification stage.*

> **Definition:** to make official or valid; to give a definite shape or form to

generalize: *They are also unable to generalize the findings to all secondary students.*

> **Definition:** to make generally applicable; to form general conclusions

glean: *The authors gleaned various ideas and insights from these three works.*

> **Definition:** to assemble or get together; to learn or find out

initiate: *The team was also responsible for initiating discussions with private firms.*

> **Definition:** to begin or introduce; to originate

scrutinize: *Leung (2003, 2004) scrutinized the material conditions in which the texts were produced.*

> **Definition:** to examine or observe deeply and critically

simplify: *Din (2001) simplifies the process by providing a structure to formulate strategic plans.*

Definition: to make easier to understand; to make clearer and less complex

strive: *Silver (1969) strives to equate her appearance with a desire to seek spiritual perfection.*

Definition: to make great effort; to try hard

Verbs that make a weak or uncertain claim

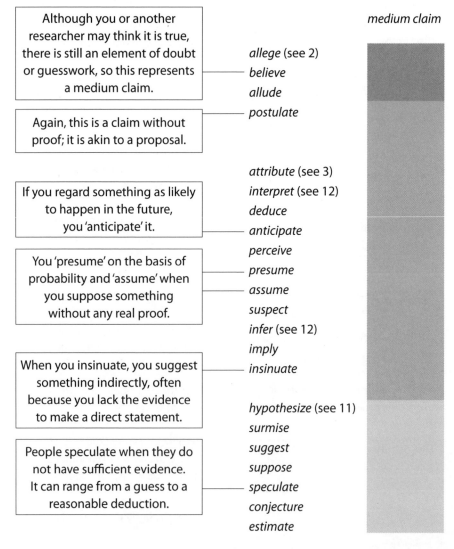

		medium claim
Although you or another researcher may think it is true, there is still an element of doubt or guesswork, so this represents a medium claim.	*allege* (see 2) *believe* *allude*	
Again, this is a claim without proof; it is akin to a proposal.	*postulate*	
If you regard something as likely to happen in the future, you 'anticipate' it.	*attribute* (see 3) *interpret* (see 12) *deduce* *anticipate*	
You 'presume' on the basis of probability and 'assume' when you suppose something without any real proof.	*perceive* *presume* *assume* *suspect* *infer* (see 12) *imply*	
When you insinuate, you suggest something indirectly, often because you lack the evidence to make a direct statement.	*insinuate*	
People speculate when they do not have sufficient evidence. It can range from a guess to a reasonable deduction.	*hypothesize* (see 11) *surmise* *suggest* *suppose* *speculate* *conjecture* *estimate*	

educated guess

Ten more verbs of interest

Here are ten more effective verbs that have been selected for their usefulness and the frequency with which they occur in academic writing. Obtain a definition, locate some examples of usage, and start employing them in your writing!

accompany   *mediate*
authorize   *retain*
demarcate   *retrieve*
illuminate   *stipulate*
marginalize   *underscore*

23 ADJECTIVES: Evaluative adjectives

Adjectives for expressing that something is important or useful

These adjectives are used when something is considered **important** or **highly regarded**. See also the following terms from Part A: definitive (6), desirable (7), fundamental (10), instrumental (12), integral (12), and prominent (16).

advanced: *Access to advanced technology proves difficult in remote areas.*

> **Explanation:** see 1, 'advanced'

compelling: *Despite the fact that conditionality arguments seem compelling, it is debatable how effective these strategies actually are.*

> **Explanation:** implies that something really captures the attention and is hard to ignore

dynamic: *Dynamic capabilities can benefit the individual and the organization as a whole.*

> **Explanation:** means that something is innovative and unique, or constantly in motion and changing

empowering: *The programme is designed to be empowering for women and self-employed people.*

> **Explanation:** uplifting and enabling, usually used for suppressed or minority groups

enduring: *The strong relationship between customers and the brand derives from its distinct and enduring traits.*

> **Explanation:** implies lasting or remaining for a long time, often because of a strong bond or feature

enhanced: *Yen (2009) argued that learning is enhanced when there are enough reference materials.*

> **Explanation:** used when something has been improved, usually in intensity or appeal; see also 9, 'enhance'

exceptional: *The purpose of the clause was to provide immunity in the agreed exceptional circumstances.*

> **Explanation:** means far beyond what is normal either because it is excellent or rare/unusual

influential: *The networking allowed access to a larger group of executives and influential public figures.*

> **Explanation:** something that exerts an influence; it can be important in a field or persuasive to people

innovative: *This type of decision-making occurs when the situation is very complex, important, or requires an innovative procedure.*

> **Explanation:** implies that something is new, different, exciting or experimental

notable: *The financial crisis in 2008 had a notable influence on Chinese firms' capital structures.*

> **Explanation:** worthy of notice; used when something is prominent or memorable and is a formal word for noticeable

noteworthy: *It is noteworthy that a resemblance exists between the rules in the US and those in the UK.*

> **Explanation:** similar in meaning to notable but might not have the acknowledged greatness or importance that notable implies

pivotal: *Political factors can play a pivotal role in the education of women.*

> **Explanation:** of crucial importance and often relates to a particular moment or event

profound: *Their opinions and decisions have profound influence from Latin America to Africa on addressing these transnational challenges.*

> **Explanation:** depth or intensity of thought or action; often relates to complex thinking

stellar: *A positive political environment and stellar economic performance are the ultimate goals of these host countries.*

> **Explanation:** quite an informal word for outstanding or important; often used for dramatic effect or for marketing/advertising purposes

strategic: *Its strategic position in the globalized economy remains.*

> **Explanation:** important or essential, usually in relation to tactics or the benefits it might bring

unprecedented: *There was a major boom in the housing market in the late 1980s, and then a bust occurred on an unprecedented scale.*

> **Explanation:** having no previous example or not seen before

valuable: *Marketers should try to accumulate valuable data from customers at this stage.*

> **Explanation:** apart from the monetary definition, it can mean worthwhile or irreplaceable

vital: *The study of motivation is vital for a complete understanding of these different emotions.*

> **Explanation:** necessary and essential; without it, something else cannot happen or be a success.

This next set of adjectives can be used when something is considered **useful** or **relevant**. See also applicable (2), authentic (3), beneficial (3), coherent (4), salient (18), and viable (20).

accessible: *There can be no education services without accessible information for these disadvantaged groups.*

> **Explanation:** easily understood and clear, or easily obtained

appropriate: *The next stage is formulation, where the speakers decide how to use appropriate grammatical markers.*

> **Explanation:** right, correct or suitable for the task

capable: *Only two of the prospective employees were considered capable.*

> **Explanation:** can mean either having the ability to do something, or being generally competent and reliable

compatible: *But are these teaching modes compatible with thinking skills?*

> **Explanation:** describes two things that are able to exist with each other or are a good match or combination

competitive: *These subsidiaries indirectly create a competitive atmosphere in the host countries' markets.*

> **Explanation:** for people, a strong desire to compete or succeed; for a product, value for money or low in price

constructive: *The game narrative has a format that is constructive and sequential.*

> **Explanation:** helpful and useful when relating to comments or criticism; also means promoting further development

credible: *This method will assist the researcher in acquiring credible data suitable for the research aims.*

> **Explanation:** trustworthy or effective/capable

distinct: *The EU is suggested to be a normative power that is distinct from other organizations.*

> **Explanation:** clear and definite (*distinct improvement*), or different (*distinct from*)

distinctive: *The main reason would be that distinctive tax systems exist in different nations.*

> **Explanation:** similar to distinct but also implies that something has a special quality that makes it easily recognizable

favourable: *Moreover, this embeddedness creates favourable conditions for high-tech firms.*

> **Explanation:** helpful (*favourable environment*), or encouraging and positive (*favourable review*)

legitimate: *However, Muldoon (2001) stated that an insider may be seen only as a facilitator rather than as a legitimate researcher.*

> **Explanation:** either lawful, or reasonable and valid (*legitimate concerns*)

motivational: *The motivational effects of a fully functional learning environment should be formally studied.*

> **Explanation:** relates to providing an incentive or reason for doing something

opportune: *It was an opportune time to brief the participants on the tasks.*

> **Explanation:** means either happening at the right time, or suitable for a particular purpose

productive: *The island was said to be fertile and productive of every crop.*

> **Explanation:** either favourable and fertile (*productive land*) or creative and hard-working (*productive employee*)

progressive: *Learning usually happens in a progressive manner.*

> **Explanation:** means moving forward or advancing. Can be used for someone with new or unique ideas.

responsive: *Because there is a trend towards increased competition over time, marketing must be responsive to life-cycle changes.*

> **Explanation:** reacting positively and readily to change, stimulus, or new ideas

symbolic: *The governor's role is more often symbolic than actually managerial.*

> **Explanation:** representative or serving as an example of a particular situation or form (sometimes used to describe a role or position that lacks any real purpose or requirement as in the example given).

valid: *At least 140 valid observations had to be obtained for a bias-free estimation.*

> **Explanation:** can mean well founded and justified (*valid concerns*), effective (*valid response*), or lawful (*valid contract*)

Adjectives for expressing that something is negative, unimportant, or unnecessary

Methods, ideas, and systems without (*devoid of*) any positive attributes and that can only be evaluated negatively (*adverse, deleterious, damaging, detrimental*) are uncommon. Usually when something is portrayed in a negative light, it simply has more weaknesses than strengths.

Something may be lacking in scope (*insufficient*), or scale (*inadequate*), previous investigation or foundation (*experimental*), or outcome and delivery (*ineffective*). It may be too basic in concept or technology (*primitive*) or prone to error (*unreliable*) or issues (*problematic*), which would make it *questionable*. If it is unpredictable (*volatile*) or hard to discover (*elusive*), this may restrict the argument or its application (*limiting, constraining, restrictive*), thus *disrupting* the process. Conversely, something may be too stable and foreseeable (*predictable*), making it no more than *functional* and perhaps even unoriginal. It may even be considered of secondary importance (*peripheral*), lacking any real importance (*trivial, inconsequential*) or largely irrelevant (*immaterial*).

■ EXAMPLES

devoid: *The house soon lost its fittings and is now devoid of decoration.*

adverse: *The scale is further translated into significance of impact (either adverse or beneficial) ranging from 'neutral' to 'very high'.*

insufficient: *The textbooks are insufficient, and even the tutor's notes are vague.*

experimental: *The conclusion that different experimental arrangements would eventually solve the problem seems flawed.*

primitive: *Music was used throughout but was rather primitive in structure and composition.*

problematic: *See 16, 'problematic'.*

questionable: *Li (2004) only used a sample of 40, so the effectiveness is questionable.*

elusive: *The blueprint is suitable, but results remain elusive due to the following constraints.*

limiting: *These guidelines are limiting because they do not allow for flexible interpretation of roles.*

trivial: *Any of the scenarios can amount to the unseaworthiness of a vessel, ranging from trivial (scenarios 2, 3) to serious (scenarios 1, 4).*

immaterial: *First, it reaffirmed that any deviation, no matter how slight or immaterial, constituted a fundamental breach of contract.*

Time, frequency, and order adjectives

You may have plenty of time (*ample*) or been able to extend or lengthen the time to do something (*protracted, prolonged*). There could be very little time (*minimal*; see 13) or not enough time (*insufficient*), or it may have come and gone very quickly (*transient*). Something could be likely to happen soon (*prospective*; see 16) or it may have started and is ongoing (*continual, persistent*; see 15). An event may happen regularly (*periodic, repeated, intermittent*), at least once more (*recurrent*) or unpredictably (*sporadic*). Events can occur in a sequence (*sequential*) that is uninterrupted (*successive, consecutive*) or happen at the same time (*simultaneous, concurrent, synchronous*).

Ten more adjectives of interest

Here are ten more effective adjectives that have been hand-picked for their use-fulness and the frequency with which they occur in academic writing. Obtain a definition, locate some examples of usage and start employing them in your writing!

analogous	*nuanced*
archetypal	*overriding*
deep-seated	*prerequisite*
exacting	*rigid*
impromptu	*stringent*

24 ADVERBS: Linking adverbs and sentence adverbs

Some adverbs are employed at the start of a sentence and modify the entire sentence. These are called sentence adverbs or adverbials (e.g., *Inevitably, these economic policies will only satisfy those who . . .*). Only certain adverbs can be used in this way, and the most useful ones are featured in this section. An effective sentence adverb will add some explanation to what follows rather than just act as a meaningless linking word. Note that the adverbs in this chapter can also be used mid-sentence and between two commas following a modal or an auxiliary verb (e.g., *Adopting certain economic policies is, inevitably, a result of . . .*).

Adverbs that are used as intensifiers

These adverbs are used to express something with force or certainty.

doubtless: *Doubtless, the directors will buy when they are certain, and therefore purchases can be treated as a positive signal.*

> **Definition:** certainly, surely; presumably

crucially: *Crucially, parents can be brought together to meet the needs of the child.*

> **Definition:** significantly; very importantly

inevitably: *Inevitably, adopting certain economic policies is dictated by the economic situation itself.*

> **Definition:** certain to happen; predictably

notably: *Notably, several other countries are considering legislation while other developing economies are beginning to recognize the need to develop board-level talent.* (See also 13.)

> **Definition:** particularly; especially; prominently

overwhelmingly: *Overwhelmingly, the major hurdle impinging on EU activities proved to be finance.*

> **Definition:** greatly, completely; incapable of being resisted

undoubtedly: *Undoubtedly, this will involve a shift in the mindset of the educators.* (See 20.)

Definition: certainly; unquestionably

Adverbs that are used as restrictives

These adverbs are used to add caution to a claim, limit the extent of the claim, or clarify a previous comment.

admittedly: *Admittedly, there is a difference in the use of graphics in their annual reports.*

Definition: by acknowledgement; willingly conceded

allegedly: *Allegedly, they were offered a $90 million cash bribe for a contract that involved constructing a gas plant.*

Definition: reportedly; supposedly

evidently: *Evidently, it affected the US policy towards US-Sino relations.*

Definition: seemingly, apparently

Usage notes: When used directly before the verb it can be considered an intensifier, presenting a more definite claim akin to clearly or obviously. (*This evidently changed when the new regulations came into force*).

indirectly: *Indirectly, the negative relationship between interest rates and commodity returns is revealed.*

Definition: not directly or in a straight manner

primarily: *Primarily, this is used with coded data and split into categories.* (See 16.)

Definition: chiefly; mainly

principally: *Principally, companies must try to be socially responsible to improve their reputation.*

Definition: mainly; most importantly

Adverbs of manner that are effective as conjunctives and sentence adverbs

Some adverbs that begin sentences as adverbials may also be used to link two independent clauses. When an adverb does this, it is termed a conjunctive. A conjunctive will always follow a semicolon and then take a comma. (*The students can begin writing as soon as they are given the booklet; alternatively, they can plan and sketch for ten minutes on rough paper.*)

To create a suitable link (conjunctive) or to provide context for the upcoming sentence (sentence adverb), the appropriate adverb will need to be identified.

You may want to form a contrast (*conversely*), state a contradiction (*paradoxically*), or express another possibility (*alternatively*). You may be considering similarities (*correspondingly*) or similarities and differences (*comparatively*). You can state something clearly (*explicitly*), officially (*formally*), or with a more imaginative and nonliteral meaning (*figuratively*).

You may want a link that shows that the action in the first part had the expected effect (*predictably*), is likely to have that effect (*invariably, logically*), actually had an unexpected result (*inadvertently, unwittingly*), or has led to a prediction (*presumably*). You can also emphasize the importance of a point (*critically*) or clarify what this could actually mean (*technically, theoretically*).

■ EXAMPLES

paradoxically: *Paradoxically, their focus on only the current regime inspired this research project on the origins of the movement.* (See also 14, 'paradox'.)

correspondingly: *Correspondingly, Son et al. (2010) developed an alternative specification to deal with this issue.*

comparatively: *Comparatively, Participant C grew up in a peaceful domestic environment.*

explicitly: *Explicitly, we address the phenomenon from a dynamic perspective.* (See also 9, 'explicit'.)

predictably: *The feedback was then catalogued; predictably, the responses on the outcomes of the process vary across member states.*

invariably: *Invariably, a well-designed programme will have an impact on teaching and learning practices.*

inadvertently: *Inadvertently, this has served to marginalize Third-World women.*

presumably: *The work uses very abstract imagery; presumably, the writer is a painter or artist of some description.*

technically: *Technically, this cannot be considered an example of the genre.*

theoretically: *Theoretically, these zones should be free from complex bureaucracy.* (See also 19, 'theoretical'.)

Time, frequency, and order adverbs

Not all of the adverbs below can be employed at the start of sentences or clauses, but they are useful for detailing the time and frequency of an action. Use the adverb in brackets when you want to report . . .

something that happens in an independent manner or without intention (*automatically*)

things that happen in time order (*chronologically*)

something that has no limit or end (*endlessly*)

something that is related to a past event (*retrospectively*)

something that happens usually because of habit or custom (*habitually*)

something that happens in an expected manner (*routinely*; see 18)

something that happens in intervals (*intermittently, periodically*)

something that happens for a short or limited time (*temporarily*)

something that happens just for an instant or very soon (*momentarily*)

something that is never-ending (*perpetually*)

something that happens early or before the proposed time (*prematurely*)

something that happens first or at the start (*initially*)

something that is happening now (*presently*)

something that happens with little or no delay (*promptly*)

something that happens next or after something else (*subsequently*; see 19)

something that happens in a consecutive manner (*sequentially, successively*)

things that happen at the same time (*simultaneously*)

something that happens that has not been planned (*spontaneously*)

Ten more adverbs of interest

Here are ten more effective adverbs that have been hand-picked for their useful-ness and the frequency with which they occur in academic writing. Obtain a defi-nition, locate some examples of usage and start employing them in your writing!

aptly	*profoundly*
consciously	*remotely*
exclusively	*substantively*
extensively	*succinctly*
overtly	*vividly*

25 WORDS for unity and division

This section looks at terms used to express connected actions and the strength of those connections. It also features terms used to describe things that are being united and divided and the most effective words for showing contrast between ideas or stances.

When someone's belief or stance is in agreement with someone else's

If people's ideas are in agreement or their stance on a particular issue matches, we can say they *concur* or have found *commonality*. They may have a personal *affinity* with each other or an affinity for each other's ideas. Perhaps a *rapport* has built up over time or an *accord* has formed because of their *compatibility*.

Positions that were not similar at the start but are now finding agreement are reported as *converging*, *aligning*, or *orienting*. If one party was forced to change or decided to change his or her opinions, then that person is *complying* or becoming *compliant*. Sometimes, one party just has to back down and *conform*. It could be that he or she needed to *coordinate* ideas or operations to form a *collective* for *mutual* benefit. *Concordance* is sometimes necessary so things are equal, thus creating *parity* between those involved.

■ EXAMPLES

concur: *Cheng and Hu (2008) concur and add that poor levels of literacy are associated with low-income or unemployed groups.*

affinity: *It is clear from Table 2.4 that group three has a strong affinity for rote learning.*

rapport: *Good rapport developed among the people involved in the workshops.*

orienting: *Once the communities interact, orienting the teaching towards individual identity will take place.*

compliant: *... whereas superiors take less or no notice and sometimes even force subordinates to be compliant.*

coordinate: See 6.

concordance: *The division between functions, properties, and means seems to be in concordance with these aims of software engineering.*

parity: *Fraser holds the view that a status model could alter the procedures that impede parity.*

When one action or purpose has a connection to another

intertwined: *Because these narratives are intertwined, it is difficult to properly assess them separately.*

Usage notes: In figurative writing, narratives are most commonly said to intertwine.

convergence: *The convergence of these actions will result in greater progress.*

Usage notes: The adjective (*convergent*) and verb forms (*converge* and its present participle, *converging*) are also much used in academic writing. *These technologies are rapidly converging . . .*

complementary: *Their complementary skills set allowed them to complete the task efficiently.*

Usage notes: When actions or skills are complementary, they may actually be different. Complementary means that they enhance the qualities of the other and therefore form a good union.

connectedness: *There was a sense of connectedness with previous events.*

Usage notes: Connectedness should be used instead of connectivity when there is merely an association or a feeling of being close to something. Connectivity is usually used when objects or devices are physically connected to each other.

equivalent: *This qualification was set in 2005 and is the equivalent of the British GCE 'A' levels.*

Usage notes: See 9, 'equivalent'.

concomitant: *Reduced levels of compliance are expected to be concomitant with a less stringent strategy.*

Usage notes: A more formal and academic way of saying occurring together or associative, concomitant implies a natural pairing and is employed in the medical sciences for 'dose', 'treatment', and 'diseases'.

The following terms are helpful for demonstrating how strong a link or connection is.

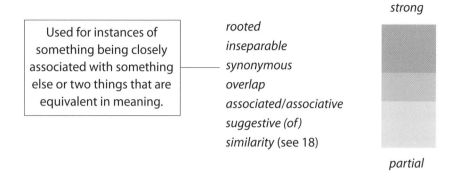

strong

Used for instances of something being closely associated with something else or two things that are equivalent in meaning. — *rooted*
inseparable
synonymous
overlap
associated/associative
suggestive (of)
similarity (see 18)

partial

When something joins something else to work together or to form a whole

Following on from the terms earlier that detailed agreement between parties, this conversation will focus on situations where two things combine to create one entity. This might be figuratively (ideas or theories combining) or meant in a more literal sense (for instance, two companies merging).

When ideas, features, or elements come together they can be said to *fuse* or *synthesize*, taking words from science to figuratively describe a perfect *union*. *Synergy* can then take place, meaning that the powers of the combined 'two' are greater and more effective than when they were working independently. *Coalescence* often implies a more gradual process in forming the union, while a *hybrid* is an entity created from two distinct elements. Ideas or features can be *embedded* or *blended* into more complete forms, whereas information and physical structures tend to be *appended*, *annexed*, or *adjoined* to something that is larger. When an entity joins to another (often larger entity) it is *incorporated* into it or *assimilated* into it if the new circumstances involve a group or society. Two fairly equal powers may form an *alliance* and *collaborate*, but this does not necessarily mean they become one, whereas an *amalgamation* does.

■ EXAMPLES

synthesize: *The company provides customers with an experience that synthesizes the worlds of fashion, technology, and music.*

synergy: *The lack of official cooperation between them prevented any real synergy from occurring.*

coalescence: *In the paper, the coalescence of these granules is demonstrated.*

embedded: *Intangible resources are physically invisible, such as reputation built over time and knowledge embedded in the organization.*

adjoin: *The firm adjoined these points to the document and then re-sent the contracts.*

assimilate: *These managers may find it more difficult to assimilate large targets into a combined entity.*

collaborate: *The organization also collaborates with charitable trusts to ensure young workers are given opportunities.*

When ideas or positions are opposing or in contrast with each other

Sometimes ideas and viewpoints are *dissimilar* or *disparate*. They may have some differences (*variance*; see 20) or be clearly different (*distinct*). If two ideas have the same origin or characteristics but then move away from each other (*divergence*), they are said to be *diverging*. This leads to a *dissociation* and means they have become *detached*. A *dichotomy* may then occur, which is a division with two opposing units. If they are still together but are formed of dissimilar components, they are considered *heterogeneous*. If these dissimilar parts are unsuitable, then *incongruity* occurs. When standpoints or positions are opposing, they are said to be *conflicting* and *discordant*, which leads to *discord*. Most topics and debates produce *diverse* opinions; some are complete opposites (*polar/polarity*) and would never be able to form an alliance (*incompatible*). These divisions will then cause those that hold one view to *rebuke* or *reproach* the other.

■ EXAMPLES

disparate: *Misinterpretation can generally be blamed on the disparate understanding and employment of the terminology.*

distinct: *It briefly summarizes the distinct characteristics of this duty within each regime.*

diverging: *Some of these markets are diverging due to economic and cultural diversity.*

dichotomy: *Therefore, as Khan (2001) suggests, within the context of this centre-periphery dichotomy, the party should have a positive view.*

conflicting: See 4.

discordant: *The meeting was surprisingly friendly and not a single discordant word was uttered by either party.*

When something splits from something else or is broken up into parts

disperse: *The more dispersed the equity of the firm, the more liquidated the stock.*

Synonyms: scattered, separate, spread, distribute

diffusion: *The diffusion of this innovation is mainly achieved through interactive networks.*

Synonyms: expansion, dissemination

diversify: *Suddenly, India realized that it needed to diversify its trading partner base and look beyond the Soviet Union.*

Synonyms: vary, transform, expand, branch out

fragment (verb): *There is a tendency for analysis to fragment the data.*

Synonyms: split, split up, break, break up, divide

proliferate: *As firms exchange data with their trading partners, it proliferates the risk due to the sensitivity of the information shared.*

Synonyms: expand, increase, multiply

ramify: *The veins ramify to meet their extremities in order to receive the blood.*

Synonyms: branch, fork, divide, separate, split

segmented: *They introduced a marketing process whereby candidates are segmented with a view to being attracted and persuaded.*

Synonyms: divided, subdivided, broken up

segregated: *The early schools for children with impairments were segregated, and there was no real formal education in rural areas.*

Synonyms: separated, isolated, set apart, singled out

stratification: *Education is seen as the solution to eliminate racial and social stratification.*

Synonyms: layering, arrangement, division, categorization

26 WORDS for fact and fabrication

The importance of word selection is never more evident than when you wish to express a fact or make a claim. Unless there is compelling evidence of something and experts or society have accepted it as given or standard, the general advice is to err on the side of caution. This section explores the terms to use for the varying degrees of fact and fiction recognized in your own study and that of others.

When something is accepted as true or there is certain evidence

There are two occasions when definitive language can be used for claiming something: first, when it is considered fact or when those in the relevant field assume it to be true; second, when conclusive evidence has been found by a researcher or by you and is being presented to the reader.

Truths that require no proof because experience has confirmed them (*axioms* and *truisms*) can be distinguished from those rules or principles generally uttered by authority figures (*dictums* and *maxims*). So, we can say things with *certainty* or *definitively* if they are *accepted, acknowledged,* or *trusted.* You may have *indisputable* or *conclusive* evidence which *undoubtedly* confirms a theory. Something may be *unmistakably* clear, or receive *unequivocal* support or be *unquestionably* occurring. Remember that these terms may also be disproving something emphatically. You may be unequivocally wrong, or something may prove to be unquestionably bad.

Once you have *confirmation* or have proven something with sufficient evidence, you can then look for ways to announce this. Your research may have *demonstrated* or *confirmed* something you proposed, or you may have *substantiated, verified, validated,* or *corroborated* the work of others. If you do succeed, then you can say your efforts were *vindicated.*

■ EXAMPLES

definitively: See 6, 'definitive'.

acknowledged: *These injustices in the early cases have now been acknowledged.*

undoubtedly: See 20, 'undoubtedly'.

substantiate: *Researchers examine the meaning of data and redirect observation to substantiate those meanings in the field.*

corroborate: *He emphasized reflective thinking that brings to light further facts in order to corroborate or reject a belief.*

When you believe or someone believes it is likely to be true

Choosing the correct term when there is likelihood or partial evidence is usually more complicated than when there is conclusive evidence or, conversely, when something is clearly untrue or just guesswork. The following list explores that grey area between confirmed and conjectured.

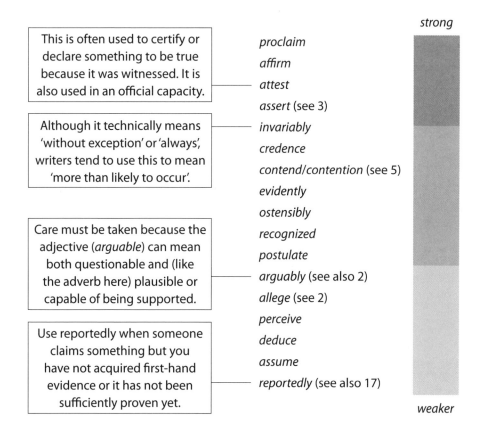

This is often used to certify or declare something to be true because it was witnessed. It is also used in an official capacity.	*proclaim* *affirm* *attest* *assert* (see 3)	**strong**
Although it technically means 'without exception' or 'always', writers tend to use this to mean 'more than likely to occur'.	*invariably* *credence* *contend/contention* (see 5) *evidently* *ostensibly*	
Care must be taken because the adjective (*arguable*) can mean both questionable and (like the adverb here) plausible or capable of being supported.	*recognized* *postulate* *arguably* (see also 2) *allege* (see 2)	
Use reportedly when someone claims something but you have not acquired first-hand evidence or it has not been sufficiently proven yet.	*perceive* *deduce* *assume* *reportedly* (see also 17)	**weaker**

When you believe or someone believes there is doubt or insufficient evidence

This conversation reveals terms that can be used when there is doubt about the claims and when the method or process was not effective enough to produce sufficient evidence.

Some studies lack focus and use *vague* or *imprecise* methods, which leads to *indeterminate* or *inconclusive* evidence. Studies that lack purpose and consistent elements will therefore create *disparity* and *ambiguity*. Claims may then be *spurious* or *speculative*, even *idealized*. A researcher can *allege* something that *seemingly* or *purportedly* shows something, but without the evidence or a suitable process it will be *questionable, debated*, and *disputed*.

A claim may be made that is too narrow and only relevant in certain situations (*circumstantial*), or it may have come about through personal observation or random investigation (*anecdotal*). When generalized to a wider population or different field, these *hypothetical* scenarios will lead to or be identified as *assumption, supposition, speculation* (see 18), and *conjecture*.

It is advisable to proceed with *caution* (or be *cautionary*) when assessing claims and making them. Being *skeptical* or tentative is always preferable to jumping in and endorsing something—or announcing findings as the gospel truth!

■ EXAMPLES

indeterminate: *It is these indeterminate laws that are less likely to be obeyed, because they often go unpunished when violated.*

disparity: See 8, 'disparity'.

ambiguity: See 2, 'ambiguity'.

speculative: *The notion that this was designed to weaken the smaller companies, making them vulnerable to foreign buyers, is merely speculative (Lin 2009).*

seemingly: *Several of the reports seemingly have pro-government agendas.*

purportedly: *The unpublished document purportedly contains evidence that fraudulent activity took place between 1978 and 1981.*

questionable: *It is questionable whether the provision would apply to the carrier of the goods.*

supposition: *This supposition is inconsistent with Dalem et al. (2006), who demonstrated that takeovers in this industry are frequent.*

cautionary: *Because of the hype about the possible findings, the authors felt the need to provide some cautionary notes.*

skeptical: *They were more skeptical of the EU report than were the core members of the party.*

When there is evidence that something is clearly false

This first set of terms can be employed when the researcher or writer has clearly misled the reader. These are strong claims and are accusatory. It is essential that clear evidence be provided if alleging that someone has exaggerated the truth or something is imaginary.

convinced
their claims
are false

fabricate/fabrication
falsify
fraudulent

used to refer to evidence or results that have been changed in order to deliberately mislead

manufactured
deceptive
distort
pretence

used for when slightly altering findings, facts, or motives to change the intended meaning or to make favourable or unfavourable

Here, there is clear evidence that the researcher's claims (or methods) are simply false (or wrong).

erroneous/erroneously
flawed
inaccuracy/inaccurate
invalid

used for a process or technique that has a defect or contains mistakes; usually a result of poor reasoning or application

When the claims seem to be exaggerated or are likely to be false, these terms can be used.

disregarded
unfounded
implausible
fanciful
unsupported
unreliable/unreliability

used when a claim has been exaggerated or an idea is impractical; it is not based on fact but imagination instead

unrealistic
untested
scarcely
unsubstantiated

used instead of barely and hardly and as a negative to mean 'probably not' or 'by no means'

unconvinced
their claims
are true

Report the fallacy

You can report disagreement or dismissive actions by using one of the following verbs:

decry, denounce, deride, discredit, dispel, disprove, rebuke, refute

decry*: Hang (2004) decried the lack of support from local authorities.*

denounce*: Many policies were implemented and denounced in a short period, just because they had not come from the parent company.*

deride*: They were derided for their thoughtless approach to a sensitive area.*

discredit*: An attempt was made to discredit these researchers and their findings.*

dispel*: With these results, we are therefore able to dispel the hype surrounding this technique.*

disprove*: The third objective is to finally disprove this long-held theory.*

rebuke*: Those who had delivered the report reflecting their concerns were roundly rebuked by the government.*

refute*: The next section reveals which of the contending hypotheses have been refuted.*

27 WORDS for change

Change is a common theme running through almost every type of text, so selecting the right term to express the type of change and level of change taking place is crucial for projecting the desired meaning.

Change to a trend or to circumstances

Change typically involves speed, scale, direction, or desirability.

If change is seen, it is therefore *perceptible* or *discernible*. It may be *evident* or *palpable* to some and *undetected* or *unobserved* by others. When change is *appreciable*, it is *marked* and *significant*. It may have happened quickly (*accelerated*) or emerged gradually and *steadily* (see 18), whereby it could be *intensifying*, *deepening*, or *mounting*. It can take place in stages (*graduated*, *incremental*) but if it develops (*evolves*) and widens its influence (*expands*), then things can *escalate*. The change may be continuous (in a state of *flux*), lasting, permanent (*sustained/ sustainable*), or only temporary (*transitory*).

Change may cause circumstances or trends to move in a different direction (*deviate*, *shift*) or in many directions (*dispersed*), and the level of change may occur in different degrees over time (*fluctuate*, *oscillation*, *variance*; see 20). This change might be difficult to assess (*unpredictable*).

Once change has occurred, there may be no return to the former state or conditions (*irreversible*). Change that affects things negatively can lead to the *degradation* or *deterioration* of something. Things may lose their influence or abundance and become *diminished* and *depleted*, causing *repercussions*.

■ EXAMPLES

discernible: *This would only be discernible to experienced workers.* (See also 7, 'discern'.)

appreciable: *Enterprise will build a positive image in the consumers' minds and then bring appreciable profits.*

marked: *There is a marked difference between the scores of the two groups.*

accelerated: *The economic crisis accelerated this trend, and now many SMEs operate with difficulty.*

mounting: *They studied the mounting uncertainty within this industry.*

escalate: *A competent worker should anticipate problems and organize solutions before the problems escalate to a crisis.*

flux: *Hong Kong is in a constant flux of external influence that requires continuous adaption.*

transitory: *Most of the partnerships in projects of this type are transitory.*

deviate: *The only uncertainty is whether the economy will deviate from the path policymakers expect.*

oscillation: *This is due to the oscillation of the eyes being both horizontal and vertical.*

diminished: *The report also agreed with the reasons for the diminished role of the private sector.*

Actively making a change to something

As well as those in the top 200 that indicate a change (amendment, 2; enhance, 9; incorporate, 11; integrate, 12; intensify, 12), the following represent examples of change having been initiated. Common collocates (words often found alongside the term) have been listed to provide an understanding of the situations in which to use these useful words of change.

alteration: *The alteration of brand name and logos may also damage brand equity.*

Often used with habitat, landscape, pattern, structure, function, parameters

augment: *Roomware is a concept attempting to apply computational power to augment the usability of physical objects at the expense of traditional computers.*

Often used with learning, effects, income, capacity, capability, desire

curb: *It is feared that the new regulation will curb the growth of online sales.*

Often used with efforts, emissions, violence, violations, incidence, influence, behaviour, expenditure

curtail: *It indicates that firms with high liquidity have the capacity to issue more short-term debt to curtail the agency problem.*

Often used with activities, services, efforts, ability, production, ambitions

distort: *The analyses that we extract are likely to narrow and distort the overall nature of our experience.*

> **Often used with** meaning, facts, reality, perceptions, picture

edit (verb): *The document will take considerable time to edit.*

> **Often used with** content, writing, files, video, comments, sequence

enrich: *The document data enriched these findings by providing additional information on the stages of the policymaking process.*

> **Often used with** learning, understanding, lives, experience, vocabulary

heighten: *There was concern that this would heighten the risk of financial collapse.*

> **Often used with** awareness, interest, perception, risk, concern, conflict, anxiety, fear, sensitivity

hone: *The training course is designed to hone these skills, not teach the basics.*

> **Often used with** skills, technique, ability, thinking

manipulate: *It allows dependencies and relations to be monitored and manipulated from a central entry point.*

> **Often used with** objects, variables, opinion, information, data, sounds, words, people

moderate (verb): *Their task will be to moderate the number of requests being received.*

> **Often used with** activity, effect, behaviour, impact

modification: *The survey was designed after making several revisions and modifications on those existing studies.*

> **Often used with** behaviour, effect, genetic, technique (see also 13, 'modify')

precipitate: *Thus, this carelessness may precipitate a further economic downturn for the country.*

> **Often used with** crisis, migration, conflict, violence, illness

rectify: *The technology has allowed the ship owner to communicate with the crew to rectify any problems when the crew is at sea.*

> **Often used with** situation, problem, mistake, error, shortcomings

refine: *Such categorization was further refined to identify specific points.*

> **Often used with** see 17, 'refine'.

reform: *The main reasons were macro-stability, domestic financial reforms, and globalization.*

> **Often used with** economic, political, welfare, healthcare, social

remedy (noun): *A subsequent issue is to determine which remedies will be available to the innocent party.*

> **Often used with** legal, trade, administrative, contract, medical

transpose: *The European Union transposed the provisions of the Aarhus Convention into Directive 2003/04/EC.*

> **Often used with** texts, music, messages, meaning, concept

The prefix 're-' can be used to denote change, often relating to repetition of an action, a return to a previous condition, or a correction/adjustment.

readjust	redistribution	restoration
realignment	reformulation	restructure
reappraisal	regenerate	resurgence
reassign (see 3, 'assign')	rehabilitative	rethink
recode	reorientation	retract
reconfiguration	repatriate	revert
reconstruction	replenish	revitalization
redevelopment	reposition	revive

No change to a trend or circumstance

Conditions can remain unchanged (*uniform*) for various reasons. Something may have qualities that keep it steady and uninfluenced by change (*sustainable, enduring*), or work can be undertaken to ensure conditions remain as they are (*maintain, stabilize*) if *constancy* and resistance to outside influences are sought. Change may also fail to take place due to neglect or lack of interest (*stagnation*).

■ EXAMPLES

enduring: *In his research, Stadler (2007) recognized four principles of enduring success.*

maintain: *. . . third, to develop and maintain links between the university, the placement provider, and the community.*

stabilize: *The organization attempts to stabilize the region through military and civilian interventions.*

constancy: *They looked at techniques for testing the constancy of regression relationships over time.*

stagnation: *Kenya's economy recovered from a period of stagnation in the 1990s.*

28 WORDS for amount and size

Writers of academic material must convey to the reader the scope of their topic or argument, the extent of the existing literature, the size of their sample, the frequency of their observations, etc. As with most areas of English, certain terms are used to express these elements and others are deemed inappropriate.

When stating the extent or range of something

To indicate the scope of something or its *magnitude* (which can be the extent, size, or importance; see 13), countless terms are available for conveying an expanse (*broad, comprehensive, extensive, wide-ranging*), but few satisfactorily describe a narrow range (*restricted, limited*). *Sparsely* usually relates to the population or number within an area, whereas the suffix '-wide' (*statewide, systemwide*) informs us that the range extends across the entity.

When stating the abundance of something

If a resource or entity is widespread, it is said to be *prevalent* or *profuse*. If something has spread and there are negative connotations, then *pervasive* is preferred. An *ample* supply may be said to be *replete*, but it could lead to an excess that is unnecessary (*superfluity*) and not useful (*redundancy*). An unnecessary amount is not inevitably negative, though. Where something has *amassed* to create a *plentiful* supply, this leads to an *overabundance*.

The *richness* may not be evenly spread out. It may be high in one area but low in others (*disproportionate*). If there is low abundance (*dearth*) and it is insufficient, then the resource or feature is said to be scarce, and if it has been excessively used, *depleted*.

Physical size

When stating the physical size of an object in academic English, instead of 'big' and 'large' use *considerable, substantial,* or *prominent*. Avoid enormous and gigantic. Diminutive can sometimes replace small and tiny.

■ **EXAMPLES**

scope: *The new entrants have increased their scope and developed new concepts of service.*

comprehensive: See 4, 'comprehensive'.

prevalent: See 15, 'prevalent'.

pervasive: See 15, 'pervasive'.

replete: *In this region replete with diabetes and heart disease, it is vital to reduce obesity.*

superfluity: *This superfluity continued with the creation of three more general administrative departments.*

amassed: *The main reason for the amassed resources is funding these socioeconomic projects.*

When stating quantity or amount

Using words for quantity or amount can seem simple enough, but many of the terms have specific meanings and uses. If you want to express that there is such a great number of something that it would be difficult to count, *innumerable* and *countless* are accurate selections. *Myriad* is also common for an indefinite number (even though it originally meant 10,000). *Populous* is generally limited to counting people. An *array* usually contains an element of appreciation, whereas *plethora* has the meaning of excess and therefore sometimes too many or too much—as does *surfeit*. *Surplus* also implies excess but without any real negative connotation. *Manifold* expresses a large and varied quantity, while *liberal* is restricted to the actual application of a large amount.

■ **EXAMPLES**

countless: *Furthermore, the FDI creates an enormous radiation effect and countless job opportunities for related industries.*

myriad: *There is potential for anxiety and a myriad of other negative consequences for those involved.*

array: *The ICT sector in India has experienced an array of regulatory reforms.*

surfeit: *The brief economic upturn provided the region with a surfeit of new housing.*

surplus: *It is important to investigate why firms could benefit from holding surplus cash.*

manifold: *Definitions of vulnerability are too manifold to be of use in the scenario that Leung (2011) provides.*

liberal: *I found the tutors to be liberal with their time and the advice they were willing to provide.*

When expressing the growth of something

It is often better to downplay the size or growth of something than to exaggerate; however, when the growth of something really is great we can use *considerable* and *substantial*. *Prominent* (see 16) and *appreciable* are suitable when the growth is noticeable but not necessarily impressive, while *sizeable* fits somewhere in between. The growth may be building slowly in number or amount (*growing, accruing, accumulating*) or in size (*augmenting*). Quick growth (*proliferating*) and rapid growth (*exponential*) can also sometimes be problematic (*escalating*). It may be regular and under control (*steady*) and occurring for a long time (*sustained*). Growth, therefore, can be evaluated as satisfactory (*sufficient*), ideal (*optimal*), or given a negative inference (*excessive, extreme, spiralling*).

■ EXAMPLES

considerable: See 5, 'considerable'.

substantial: See 19, 'substantial'.

appreciable: *As a consequence, today there is an appreciable difference between an individual's success and the benefits gained by the employer.*

accruing: *The competitive advantage is said to be sustainable when the firm is able to duplicate the benefits accruing from the policy.*

proliferating: *It involves the conflicting strategy of retaining the scarcity while also proliferating the product.*

escalating: *The plan was adopted and declared in 2002 due to the escalating scale of the problem.*

optimal: See 14, 'optimal'.

spiralling: *These cooperative principles are designed to address the spiralling poverty levels in the country.*

When explaining the lack of growth or negative growth

Low growth can be expressed as *minimal* or *marginal*, or if there is a particular goal or area to reach or fill, then *partial* (see 14). Partial growth can be evaluated as *insufficient, inadequate*, or *unsatisfactory*. This weak growth may be deemed *negligible* or *insignificant*, and if there is something preventing it, then *restrictive*.

Reverse growth or decay can be labelled *diminished* or *declining*. This will result in *shrinkage* in size or *reduction* in size or amount.

■ **EXAMPLES**

marginal: See 13, 'marginal'.

insufficient: *The growth of the second strain of bacteria has also been insufficient.*

negligible: *The gains were negligible, given that the initiatives were not fully developed or followed.*

restrictive: *These restrictive measures prevented the company from growing at this time.*

diminished: *An elder commands respect and enjoys these privileges so long as his or her popularity has not diminished.*

shrinkage: *Figure 4.3 reveals a decrease in urbanization accentuated by economic recession, resulting in urban shrinkage.*

29 WORDS for introducing aims and objectives

One of the hardest aspects of writing a paper or essay is writing the opening paragraph or section. It is vital that you explain to the reader why the topic is being studied and the approach being taken. This chapter provides the key vocabulary that researchers tend to use to do this.

When explaining why something is being studied

There are several possible reasons why a topic is chosen for research. The most common ones are explored in this first section.

Research may be carried out against the *backdrop* of an event or movement that is beginning (*emerging*), increasing (*escalating*), or intensifying (*deepening*). There may be an important new technique at the *forefront* of research in the field that is advantageous to study or has potential. Perhaps something is receiving attention and being well documented (*prominent*; see 16) and there is an incentive to understand and evaluate it. It may already have featured heavily in research (*prevalent*) and attracted a *profusion* of studies. Researchers and authors will strive to add to the body of literature on the subject while it is being recognized and approved (*acknowledged*) or praised (*acclaimed*)—that is, until the market becomes saturated or the event, theory, or process falls out of favour and is replaced.

You may want to study an influential or original (*seminal*) book or research that was written or carried out historically and that is receiving *renewed* interest. This *notable* work may have been *misconceived* or *neglected* or not received the *recognition* it deserved. You may want to offer a new *insight* or approach or even to contest something.

Perhaps there is a *paucity* or *scarcity* of research in the area (*under-represented*). The subject may be *underdeveloped* or even *unexplained*, and you have recognized that someone should enlighten the public, the industry or those in your chosen field.

> **Nouns for importance**
>
> To show importance, academic writers use 'foremost' for the first or most prominent, 'pinnacle' for the highest level, 'principal' for the highest in rank or position, and 'cornerstone' for the fundamental principle.

■ **EXAMPLES**

backdrop: *Against this backdrop, the study utilizes both quantitative and qualitative research methods.*

emerging: *In light of the FDI emerging from globalization, an increasing number of countries are now designing protective policies.*

deepening: *Deepening our understanding of this topic is therefore seen as critical.*

forefront: *Apple has been at the forefront of innovative technology, but the current market expansion is characterized by low-cost products.*

prevalent: See 15.

acknowledged: *These drawings are acknowledged by researchers to be a door to understanding thoughts, feelings, and experiences.*

renewed: See 17.

recognition: See 16.

paucity: *There is a paucity of up-to-date research on special education in Taiwan.*

underdeveloped: *Given the media attention, analysis of these events has been limited and arguments underdeveloped.*

When detailing the approach being taken and the nature of the research

Once the *intention* and the *premise* have been outlined at the *outset*, the next stage is to inform the reader of the approach, including the general idea (*conception*) and the extent (*scope*) and limits (*purview*) of the study. *Assertions* and *assumptions* may be outlined with any *expectations* you may have. There might have been a desire (*aspiration*) to do something or a belief (*supposition*) but then after addressing certain *considerations*, the original proposition was not *feasible*. This is where you *reassess* the *procedure* to be followed. Preliminaries such as your particular *agenda* and your *standpoint* should be revealed before commencing with the *paradigm* to be followed, the *components* to be tested or *theorized*, and the data that will be *generated*—along with any principles or philosophies *underpinning* the study or upon which the study is *grounded*.

■ **EXAMPLES**

intention: *The intention is to replicate the model in other locations to analyse the wider social impact.*

premise: See 15.

conception: See 4.

purview: *Small-scale effects fall outside the purview of this study.*

assumptions: See 3, 'assumption'.

supposition: *This study seeks to obtain data that can explore this supposition in detail.*

standpoint: *From this standpoint, we will direct our efforts on the subject of Islamic feminism.*

theorized: *A study of this concept is essential for understanding how Westernization is theorized.*

generated: *We hope there will be pedagogical implications generated from the findings of the research.* (See also 10, 'generate'.)

underpinning: *The philosophy underpinning this research is pragmatism.*

grounded: *Given these factors, the research was required to be empirically grounded.*

30 WORDS for models, data, and figures

This chapter looks at the different types of data that can be collected in a research study and the relationships that can be formed between datasets or between the type of knowledge gained (epistemology) and the real world (ontology). It also reveals how to introduce a figure or diagram and how to explain the trends and patterns that have been uncovered and recognized.

When types of data are being introduced and acquired

There are many different types of data that can be collected by a researcher. It is important that the nature of the data is explained initially, again in the methodology, and then explored thoroughly within the findings section.

Data can be *observational*, *experimental* and, if based on personal experience and/or research experience, *experiential*. The data should be thoroughly analysed to look for interesting patterns and areas (*exploratory*) before these aspects are focused on and communicated to the reader (*explanatory*). Data may have been extracted from a computer model or simulation (*computational*) or from the study of people and culture (*ethnographic*).

The dataset may involve just a single variable (*univariate*), two variables (*bivariate*), or more than one target variable (*multivariate*). *Normative* data, a set that establishes a representative value or 'norm', is different from *normalizing* the data, which involves adjusting values so they align or are made clearer. Data may be combined (*pooled*) or in a separate unit but part of a larger group (*nested*). Nominal data or data with finite values (*discrete*) are unlikely to be as objective (*quantifiable*) as interval data are.

■ EXAMPLES

experiential: *Morgan (2009) pointed out that creativity and experiential learning are key to configuring worthless resources.*

explanatory: *The case study is particularly suitable for answering explanatory 'how' and 'why' questions (Yin 2009).*

ethnographic: *Our own assumptions can produce new concepts that provide the ethnographic data.*

bivariate: *They used a bivariate estimator of the variables and concluded that the inflation rate is stationary in all the countries under study.*

normative: See 13, 'normative'.

nested: *In this study, observations over time are nested within each unit of analysis.*

discrete: See 8, 'discrete'.

When relationships are being explained

Describing the relationships within and between data sets requires knowledge of certain terms.

asynchronous: *They explored students' perceptions of their learning and produced asynchronous data (Table 4).*

> **Definition:** not occurring at the same time; not starting until something else has finished

binomial: *Other symptoms were evaluated binomially with either a yes or a no answer.*

> **Definition:** something consisting of two types, names, or terms

concurrent: *To best understand the research questions requires the concurrent collection and analysis of quantitative and qualitative data.*

> **Definition:** taking place at the same time; occurring or existing side by side

conditional: *They model the conditional variances (σ_t^2) that are the expected values of the squares of the errors (ε_t^2).*

> **Definition:** depending on other factors; not certain; true for only certain values of the variable

cyclical: *Their cyclical model of technological change was also used as a guide.*

> **Definition:** characterized by recurrence in cycles; fluctuating according to set changes in a system

deterministic: *The test can incorporate the trends in the model to assess the presence of a unit root with deterministic elements.*

> **Definition:** the behaviour of something being determined by its makeup and natural order rather than by randomness; having only one outcome

dichotomous: *According to Cohen et al. (2007), dichotomous questions are inappropriate in complex situations.*

> **Definition:** dividing into two parts; classified by two parts
>
> **Usage notes:** The term 'dyadic' can also be used to refer to a group of two. *This was applied to business settings where pure dyadic relationships are relatively scarce.*

intergroup: *Group and intergroup dynamics influence the relationship between employees and can lead to a healthy environment.*

> **Definition:** occurring between two or more groups

reciprocal: *We expect to capture the reciprocal relations between the explanatory factors and democracy.*

> **Definition:** mutual; corresponding or matching; having the same relationship

recursive: *Seidel (1988) insisted that the process is recursive because each step could warrant a return to another step.*

> **Definition:** relating to a procedure or process that can be applied repeatedly

stepwise: *This analysis was performed by a stepwise procedure from the simplest model (Model 1) to those with control variables (Models 5 and 6).*

> **Definition:** marked by a gradual progression; step by step

stochastic: *These stochastic terms, which enter the models additively, capture the shocks in the models.*

> **Definition:** involving a random process or variable

When introducing and referring to figures and data

Figures and diagrams that are presented in your work have to be introduced or referred to in the correct way. The following reporting verbs are most often used for this task and, if suitable, serve as good alternatives to 'show'. See also clarify (see 4), compile (4), denote (7), depict(ion) (7), exemplify (9), generate (10), outline (14), portray (15), and replicate (17). Note: the verb 'exhibit' cannot introduce figures and tables.

annotate: *All the actions using ELAN software have been annotated in Figure 2.2.*

append: *The actual figure is calculated separately and has been appended to Tables 3.4–3.9.*

observe: *However, this level showed a significant difference between positive and neutral conditions in all the emotional dimensions, as observed in Figure 3.2.*

perceive: *The lack of deviation can be perceived from the graph in Figure 6.*

quantify: *Once this took place, the migration levels were quantified (Table 2).*

simplify: *We have therefore taken Zheng's original framework and simplified it (Figure 7).*

tabulate: *The data were then tabulated for ease of use (Tables 3.3–3.9).*

visualize: *Once the descriptions were given, the main features were visualized by the team (Figures 5–11).*

When naming elements and describing trends

There are certain elements within statistics that may need referring to when graphically representing data. This first conversation and set of definitions will help when annotating *tabulated* and visual data.

The highest point of any object or shape is the *apex*. *Zenith* tends to be more figurative or limited to celestial observation. The 'peak' can also be used, its opposite being the *trough*. If data are divided to show where values lie, then it is usually into four parts (*quartiles*) or 100 parts (*percentiles*). Points that lie outside the normal range are *outliers* and are usually rejected as *anomalies*. Researchers will also normally reject duplicates and instead focus on *clusters*. Shapes and curves may be described as *U-shaped*, *elliptical*, or *perpendicular*. Lines may rise and fall *sharply* or gently, or remain steady and *constant*.

■ EXAMPLES

apex: *This is not the case for point v on the graph (the apex).*

percentile: *The third to fifth columns report the 5th and 95th percentiles of the posterior distribution of the parameters.*

anomalies: *The anomalies in the data are highlighted in red (Figure 3).*

elliptical: *As Figure 7.2 depicts, patients undertake a therapeutic route with an elliptical shape.*

This next part presents definitions of some more elements that relate to figures and graphs.

curvature: *Analysis begins with an interpretation of the curvature of the line.*

Definition: the degree of curving of a line or surface; the degree of (abnormal) curving of a part of the body

figuration: *Innovative approaches to figuration are common when companies report their performance.*

Definition: the general shape, form, or outline; a figurative representation

inset: *The map shows the surrounding area, and the inset reveals the exact location of the site.*

Definition: to set something inside something else; an image or illustration set within a larger one

intersection: *From Figure 16, for the curve at the intersection of IS and LM0 . . .*

Definition: the point at which two or more things meet

midpoint: *Measurements of formant frequencies using full trajectories are better than simply relying on the measurement near the midpoints.*

Definition: a position that is exactly in the middle of two extremes

oscillation: *The graphs below (Figures 2.1 and 2.2) demonstrate the oscillations on a frictionless surface.*

Definition: a steady backward and forward swinging motion about a single point; how much a function varies between its extreme values as it approaches a point

trajectory: *As depicted in Figure 8.21, these dotted lines eventually intersect within the trajectory of product performance.*

Definition: the course or path of something moving through air or another substance; a curve that cuts other curves or surfaces at the same angle

When associations and distinctions have been found

When faced with a dataset or when producing a graphical representation, the next step is to regard what is *observable*, *perceptible*, or *identifiable*. Something may be clearly evident, or you may have to *deduce* what is depicted in the figure.

When comparing data or datasets, there may be co-occurrence of patterns (*correlation*). To indicate that the connection is mutual or within/between, the prefix 'inter-' can be added to *dependent*, *connected*, and *related*. Values or trends that are regular or consistent are said to show *uniformity*; a strong match or correspondence is considered *cohesive*, which can create *robustness* (see 18, robust).

The data may be unrelated and *distinct* and the distribution or line distorted or slanted (*skewed*), asymmetric or irregular. *Inequalities* or *abnormalities* will always appear *nonlinear*, and these *disparities* tend to be clearer when the data are represented graphically.

■ EXAMPLES

perceptible: *This phenomenon is perceptible on several of the graphs.*

correlation: See 6.

interrelated: *These factors are overlapping and interrelated, so it is difficult to discuss one factor in isolation.*

uniformity: *Using these questions does ensure some degree of uniformity of data.*

cohesive: *Khan (2003) is renowned for producing cohesive datasets that can be analysed by students of the subject.*

distinct: *The aim was to create two distinct datasets.*

skewed: *These returns are more volatile, and skeweness is almost always negative, meaning distribution is skewed to the left.*

31 WORDS for interviews and questionnaires

The key elements when presenting the procedures of, and responses from, interviews and questionnaires are covered in this chapter. These elements include the process and methods chosen and skills employed to ensure accuracy and success, assessing the character and mood of the interviewee or respondent for interpreting the data, and communicating to the reader the responses and feedback that were obtained.

When explaining interview and question components

Interviews can be conducted in many ways and questions can take many forms. Synonyms are provided here to clarify some standard terms and help determine which are relevant for your study, so as to guide your methodology description.

agenda: *I reviewed the interview agenda to clarify what I was seeking to accomplish.*

Synonyms (nouns): plan, schedule, order, scheme, procedure

declarative: *These were designed to produce declarative statements from the respondents.*

Synonyms: expressive, definite, confirming, demonstrative

eligible: *The group comprised 28 obese patients eligible for bariatric surgery.*

Synonyms: fit, suitable, qualified, entitled

empirical: *This is the motivation for using empirical analysis in the study.*

Synonyms: direct, observed, first-hand, actual, factual, experimental

formalized: *The research should produce higher reliability because of this formalized question structure.*

Synonyms: structured, fixed, organized

mandatory: *The first set of questions was mandatory; then afterwards the respondents could select sections that were relevant to them.*

Synonyms: compulsory, required, obligatory

predetermined: *An unstructured interview tends to have no predetermined list of questions.*

Synonyms: agreed, set, prearranged, deliberate, fixed

prescriptive: *The process was prescriptive, the model serving as a checklist to track progress.*

Synonyms: rigid, fixed, law-based, rule-based

protocol: *Approval from the university ethics committee ensured that all protocol and procedures were adhered to.*

Synonyms: code of conduct/behaviour, custom, etiquette, propriety

rhetorical: *We will also outline the different rhetorical devices available to foster this strategy.*

Synonyms: verbal, stylistic, linguistic

Usage notes: A rhetorical question is one that does not require an answer. It is designed to make a statement. (The interviewee added: *'This is the seventh time it's happened but who's counting?'*)

rigid: *This process is not rigid and might be reviewed to create a balance that will capture most of the relevant answers.*

Synonyms: strict, fixed, set, inflexible, exact

sequential: *They highlight the benefits of simultaneous pairing (e.g., multitasking or multi-communicating) and sequential pairing (when one channel of communication is followed by another one straightaway).*

Synonyms: successive, consecutive, following, ordered

standardized: *The standardized questions do not allow respondents to explain in depth, so that can lead to misunderstanding.*

Synonyms: assimilated, regulated, ordered

verbatim: *It was important to use verbatim statements from respondents; this way the meaning would not be lost.*

Synonyms: word for word, exactly, precisely, faithfully

When discussing interview approaches and skills

The interviewer should always begin with a briefing that includes some instruction and preliminaries. These introductory or provisional statements help to clarify things for the interviewee and detail the procedure that will be followed.

To initiate proceedings, the interviewer needs to develop a *rapport* with the subject (interviewee) so *interaction* and *dialogue* can take place. This may involve preliminary (see 15) questions that are asked *informally* or *framed* in a straightforward manner. *Trustworthiness* is key to a successful interview so that the interviewee will feel unencumbered and uninhibited and respond truthfully and freely, enhancing the usefulness of the process. This needs to be *reciprocal* with no *preconceptions* from either party.

The interviewer must be *articulate* so the interviewee can *comprehend* the information and questions and then engage in discussion and *reflection*. *Clarification* may be required at certain times. Sometimes the interviewer will have to prompt the interviewee when he or she is *reticent* or meandering with responses, and *probe* (see 16) when the interviewee is being *evasive* or vague. This probing (*perseverance*) may require a degree of flexibility (*improvisation*) on the order of questions and the *phrasing* of them. These verbal modifications (*extemporizing*) or *refinements* can create *spontaneity*; the process will then *unfold* in a different way with different responses than if the original structure and plan had been *stringently* applied.

A *purposeful* and *guiding* process will help to gain more *insight* (making it *insightful*) and will assist with understanding the interviewee's actual *standpoint*, making his or her views more identifiable and *noteworthy*.

Assessing when to use trivial questions and when to ignore trivial answers is important, as is being perceptive to any *tacit* responses or any revealing *intonation*. All these things will be *observable* to an *observant* researcher. As well as the literal or *explicit* meaning of the interviewee's comments, this *subtext* and *underlying* feeling must therefore be *perceived*. The interviewer needs to think about the *subjectivity* of the responder and assess *tentative* or approximate (*speculative*) answers and potentially fabricated (*spurious*) claims. But *objectivity* is also required so as not to judge or bias the interviewee and interview in any way.

All these factors will ensure that the interview is *credible* and *reliable*.

■ **EXAMPLES**

rapport: *I avoided this problem by developing a rapport with the informants and beginning the interviews in a conversational style.*

interaction: *Some interviewees naturally relaxed more when the interaction was not so intense, and this is where the later survey proved effective.*

framed: See 10, 'frame'.

articulate: *Some of the younger workers may not be as articulate as the senior managers.* (See also 3, 'articulate'.)

reticent: *Subordinates need to communicate carefully and may be used to being reticent in front of others.*

evasive: *There are several measures to take if an interviewee is being evasive.*

phrasing: *The focus group revealed that questions 3, 4, and 7 needed better phrasing.*

tacit: *The interviews proved valuable, and in fact the tacit information revealed the hidden agendas relating to company policy.*

underlying: See 20, 'underlying'.

Assessing the interviewee's feelings or manner

Gauging the interviewee's demeanour and frame of mind in general and to certain questions will help you to better evaluate your data. This sliding scale from engaged in the interview to disinterested and evasive shows the general willingness of an interviewee to being there and to answering the questions. Naturally, some overlap occurs among the terms and definitions.

Use the terms in grey when the interviewee is

willing and engaged

expressive and lively	*animated*
speaking with certainty and directness (has)	*conviction*
involved, interested, committed	*engaged*
outgoing, willing to cooperate	*forthcoming*
open, straightforward	*frank*

ready and willing to receive questions	*receptive*
answering or replying readily	*responsive*
helpful and obliging	*cooperative*

uncertain; having mixed feelings	*ambivalent*
being careful; watchful	*cautious*
hesitant	*tentative*
discreet	*circumspect*
restrained; noncommittal	*guarded*
not participating actively; not reacting	*passive/passivity*

disinclined; lacking desire	*reluctant/reluctance*
worried, concerned	*apprehensive*
making an expression of opposition or dislike	*objection*
averse, loath to give information	*unwilling(ness)*

unwilling and disengaged

When reporting what interviewees have said

It is vital to select the correct reporting verb when detailing what the interviewees and respondents have said and written. The different shades of meaning are explained here. See elsewhere for an analysis of articulate (3), attribute (3), clarify (4), convey (6), disclose (7), elaborate (8), infer (12), interpret (12), reflect (17), and verify (20).

allege: *Interviewee C alleged that the senior management benefitted from this.*

> **Usage notes:** An interviewee alleges something when the comment cannot be proven or there is not enough evidence for the interviewer to consider it a fact. The interviewee may well believe it is true, but the interviewer must report it with caution. See also 2, 'allege'.

express: *The tutor expressed his unhappiness with the new teaching strategy.*

Usage notes: An interviewee expresses something when he or she shows or reveals something, usually with some feeling or emotion attached to it.

imply: *The other manager implied that new performers tend to immerse themselves in their roles very easily.*

Usage notes: An interviewee implies something when he or she suggests or indicates something without actually directly saying it. The interviewer then infers the meaning. Think carefully about how you evaluate indirect comments and make sure you have fully understood their meaning. 'Insinuate' can also be used but can have a negative connotation.

perceive: *Half of the respondents perceived this to be the case.*

Usage notes: An interviewee perceives something when he or she recognizes or identifies that something is taking place or has happened. It relates to judging an event and is often appropriate for the interviewer to use when writing up because, as a reporting verb, it does not make direct judgements or draw conclusions.

32 WORDS for reviewing and concluding

Assessing evidence in your literature review (such as evaluating older and current research on the topic) and in the discussion and conclusion sections (such as evaluating your own results or contribution) is one of the main components of written research. The scale below illustrates terms that express a positive evaluation, with diminishing strength of claim.

strong claim

Only use this for a result or outcome that has greatly exceeded expectations. Do not use it for a general evaluation.	*emphatic*
	overwhelming
	resounding
usually used with 'success' or 'failure' and 'victory' or 'defeat' (*This is a resounding success.*)	*proven*
	undeniable
	unquestionably
	definitive (see 6)
describes something that is conclusive, for a point that has settled an argument or for the greatest or most significant example of something	*conclusive*
	validated
	verified (see 20, 'verify')
	compelling
	demonstrable
used for evidence that is convincing and to describe arguments and problems that are urgent or arousing strong interest; also, a stronger form of 'persuasive'	*confirmatory*
	clarified
	evident
	notable (see 13, 'notably')

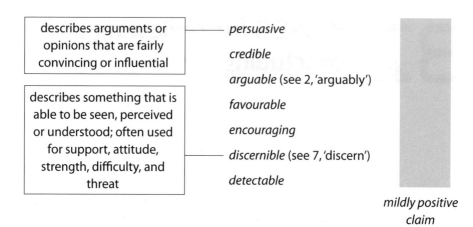

describes arguments or opinions that are fairly convincing or influential	—— *persuasive*
	credible
	arguable (see 2, 'arguably')
describes something that is able to be seen, perceived or understood; often used for support, attitude, strength, difficulty, and threat	*favourable*
	encouraging
	—— *discernible* (see 7, 'discern')
	detectable

*mildly positive
claim*

When justifying the research carried out or the results achieved

A successful study can *enhance* or *enrich* a subject and may gain *merit* from peers within the field. Your research could prove to be *useful* or *influential*. There may be some valuable *insights* or *innovative* designs produced that demonstrate *originality* and that can be *viably* reproduced or put into practice. A successful outcome *justifies* the research taking place and the effort put in. It also *vindicates* your choice of topic and the method employed.

■ EXAMPLES

enhance: See 9.

enrich: *This study has enriched the literature by using more recent data. It has also considered the application of several passive portfolio policies.*

insight: See 12.

vindicate: *The findings vindicated the decision to focus only on companies based on the peninsula.*

When expressing a negative evaluation or outcome

Sometimes a research study does not go according to plan or achieve the results anticipated. The reader is then likely to encounter the adverb *admittedly*.

The evidence may have been inadequate (*flawed*) or limited (*insufficient*), in which case it could be *discredited* or *disproved*. With unreliable evidence, the conclusions formed would be *tentative* or even *spurious*.

The research may have encountered *unanticipated* problems or had its shortcomings (*deficiencies*) exposed. Perhaps you or a researcher neglected or *overlooked* something (an *oversight*) or *miscalculated* the time it would take or an amount, or even *misinterpreted* the arguments or the data. There may have been unforeseen problems (*impediments*) or *drawbacks* that could not be overcome. Was something explored only *partially* or perhaps *omitted* (see 14) by mistake?

Evidently, the study was never going to succeed, and these *shortfalls* may be *attributable* to the fact that the process was *inhibited* by *unattainable* information or data, *restrictions* in time and ability, or *discrepancies* (see 8) between findings— or within the data extracted.

■ EXAMPLES

admittedly: *Admittedly, as the traditional products are still bestsellers they should have been emphasized.*

insufficient: *The second institution also provided insufficient data and therefore satisfactory conclusions could not be drawn.*

unanticipated: *There were some unanticipated challenges relating to the fieldwork.*

deficiencies: *Despite the above deficiencies, this study has provided some guidelines for pedagogical practice.*

oversight: *It was certainly an oversight not to have asked the patients for their views.*

drawbacks: *One of the major drawbacks was that there was nobody observing the second classroom.*

evidently: *Evidently, more time should have been set aside for this to be carried out.*

Future research

Once an evaluation of the study has been made and the limitations have been addressed, there is usually a small section dedicated to future research. Here you can offer guidance and suggestions to researchers about the areas to concentrate on or move into, perhaps building on your own study. Word selection is often dictated by the level of success or effectiveness you perceived your study to have achieved.

When the study has a positive outcome or there is optimism for studies of this nature in the future

You may be *encouraged* by the outcome of your study. The research may have set a *template* and therefore made it *reproducible*, which means that future research-ers can *replicate* your positive results if they choose to carry out the study again.

This is known as *repeatability*. Perhaps the research needs just a little *fine-tuning* or a minor *adjustment* (see 1) to make it *viable*. Sometimes the *refinement* of one aspect will produce the results you were looking to *attain*. If a further change has to be made, then a *readjustment* would be advised as long as that change is *feasible* and a result *obtainable*. Any positive result, no matter how small, *augurs* well for the future and for continued progression in the field.

If the study was less successful and had a disappointing outcome

Sometimes research and experiments do not go as planned or the results are not as expected. You may *ponder* or *reflect* on what went wrong and identify something that was *neglected*. *Hindsight* is a wonderful thing! Future researchers may need to be *mindful* or *realistic*. You may even provide several *caveats*, informing them of the need to make certain changes that you perceived as undermining the current study. *Amendments* (see 2) will have to be made. Perhaps a *re-interpretation* of an area is required. You could even suggest a complete *re-evaluation* or *reassessment* of the topic or design. This is also known as a *rethink*. Whatever the feeling is, it is always good to finish on a positive note and that, with *perseverance*, a future researcher will *prevail* if he or she heeds your advice.

■ **EXAMPLES**

reproducible: *Our model is clearly reproducible and can be used to study a wide range of experimental conditions.*

replicate: See 17.

viable: See 20.

attain: See 3.

feasible: See 10.

obtainable: *We have shown that positive results are obtainable if the correct procedure is followed.*

reflect: See 17.

mindful: *Future researchers need to be mindful of the strong cultural differences.*

caveat: *However, some caveats should be provided for future studies that focus on the local impact.*

reinterpretation: *Reinterpretation of the key actors could provide a better approach to understanding environmental protection in this area.*

Appendix: Noun collocates of the top 200

This appendix contains a selection of nouns that can be used with verbs and adjectives from the top 200 terms (these terms are written in brackets). It is presented in alphabetical order of noun.

> For example, the following top 200 terms can be employed with the noun 'ability':
>
> The students *demonstrated* their ability to . . .
> They were *equipped* with sufficient ability to . . .
> We can *utilize* the ability of the device to . . .

ability (*demonstrate, equip, utilize*)
accuracy (*verify*)
action (*decisive, emerge, encompass*)
activity (*monitor*)
age (*comparable*)
agreement (*partial*)
aim (*accomplish, consolidate*)
amount (*considerable*)
analysis (*extensive*)
answer (*definitive*)
approach (*comprehensive, coordinate, feasible, functional, persistent, robust, systematic*)
approaches (*encompass*)
approval (*generate*)
areas (*respective*)
argument (*frame, implicit, plausible*)
assessment (*comprehensive, undertake*)
assets (*consolidate*)
assumption (*theoretical*)

base (*establish*)
behaviour (*attribute, elicit, modify, normative, reinforce*)
beliefs (*elicit*)
benefit (*marginal*)
benefits (*derive, maximize*)
bias (*prone, susceptible*)

call (*growing*)
cases (*advanced*)

categories (*discrete*)
cause (*underlying*)
chance (*elaborate*)
chances (*maximize*)
change (*implement, signify*)
changes (*attribute, minimal, reflect*)
characteristics (*embody*)
choice (*hypothetical*)
clients (*prospective*)
codes (*generate*)
cohort (*prospective*)
commitment (*renewed*)
component (*integral*)
comprehension (*facilitate*)
concepts (*exploration*)
conclusion (*definitive, plausible*)
condition (*underlying*)
conditions (*optimal*)
conflict (*growing*)
consensus (*growing*)
consent (*informed*)
contribution (*decisive*)
control (*assert*)
cost (*offset*)
countries (*respective*)

damage (*susceptible*)
danger (*constitute, inherent*)

data (*comparable, compile, conflicting, constituent, disclose, generate, normative, omit, utilize, verify*)
debate (*contemporary*)
decisions (*arbitrary, endorse, informed*)
decrease (*marginal, substantial*)
degree (*advanced, complexity*)
demands (*conflicting*)
design (*refine*)
development (*facilitate*)
difference (*minimal*)
differences (*discern, fundamental, magnitude*)
difficulties (*persistent*)
discussion (*frame*)
disease (*susceptible*)

effect (*cumulative, determine, intensify, magnitude, marginal, modify, pervasive, substantial*)
effects (*manifest, monitor, offset, replicate*)
efficiency (*maximize, optimal*)
effort (*minimal, robust*)
efforts (*align*)
elements (*constituent, embody*)
emotions (*articulate*)
error (*prone*)
evaluation (*preliminary*)
evidence (*accumulate, conflicting, growing, robust*)
example (*authentic, prominent*)
experiences (*authentic*)
explanation (*plausible*)
extent (*determine, gauge*)

factor (*decisive, integral, prominent*)
facts (*omit*)
failure (*attribute*)
feature (*integral, robust, salient*)
features (*inherent*)
feelings (*articulate, intensify*)
fields (*respective*)
fieldwork (*undertake*)
figure (*prominent*)
findings (*contradictory, preliminary, replicate, verify*)
focus (*renewed*)

form (*equivalent, unified*)
framework (*coherent, comprehensive, theoretical*)
funds (*maximize*)

gains (*cumulative, maximize*)
gap (*persistent*)
goal (*accomplish*)
grade (*assign*)
growth (*comparable, optimal*)
guidance (*explicit*)
guidelines (*adhere, explicit*)

ideas (*contradictory, emerge, exploration, formulate, generate, reinforce*)
identity (*disclose*)
impact (*determine, marginal*)
implementation (*oversee*)
importance (*signify*)
improvement (*marginal, substantial*)
incidence (*cumulative*)
increase (*marginal, substantial*)
influence (*assert, contemporary, pervasive, susceptible*)
information (*acquire, authentic, clarify, compile, conflicting, convey, disclose, elicit, infer, minimal, verify*)
injury (*susceptible*)
instruction (*explicit*)
interest (*considerable, convey, gauge, generate, growing, renewed, substantial*)
interests (*align, conflicting*)
intervention (*minimal*)
investigation (*preliminary*)
issue (*frame, underlying*)
issues (*contemporary, fundamental*)

journey (*undertake*)
judgement (*arbitrary, subjective*)

knowledge (*accumulate, acquire, attain, demonstrate, enhance, equip, implicit*)

layer (*discrete*)
learning (*consolidate, facilitate, implicit, reinforce*)
lens (*theoretical*)

level (*advanced, comparable, complexity, determine, enhance, optimal*)
levels (*constituent*)
lifestyle (*modify*)
limitations (*inherent*)
list (*extensive, partial*)
lists (*compile*)
location (*desirable*)
logic (*inherent*)
loss (*cumulative, partial*)
losses (*minimal, offset*)

matters (*oversee*)
meaning (*convey, derive, elicit, refine, emerge*)
meanings (*explicit, infer*)
measure (*extensive, robust, subjective*)
message (*convey, underlying, unified*)
method (*conventional, feasible, utilize*)
methods (*discrete, respective*)
model (*contemporary, refine, theoretical, unified*)
motivation (*intrinsic*)
motive (*underlying*)
myth (*persistent*)

nature (*contradictory, fundamental, inherent, persistent, pervasive, subjective*)
need (*growing, preclude*)
needs (*functional*)
network (*comprehensive*)
number (*equivalent, growing, optimal*)

objective (*accomplish*)
opinions (*formulate, reflect*)
opportunities (*maximize*)
opportunity (*elaborate*)
optimism (*renewed*)
option (*feasible*)
outcome (*desirable*)
outcomes (*attribute, contradictory, prospective*)
overlap (*considerable*)

pain (*persistent*)
part (*integral, intrinsic*)

parts (*constituent*)
patterns (*discern*)
performance (*enhance*)
perspective (*theoretical*)
picture (*establish*)
plan (*definitive*)
plans (*coordinate, formulate, implement*)
point (*clarify, salient*)
policies (*align*)
policy (*robust*)
portrayal (*subjective*)
position (*consolidate*)
potential (*maximize*)
power (*assert, consolidate, derive, optimal*)
practice (*contemporary*)
praise (*elicit*)
pressure (*intensify*)
principles (*adhere, embody, exemplify, fundamental, guiding*)
problem (*hypothetical, magnitude*)
problems (*fundamental, manifest, persistent*)
procedures (*adhere*)
process (*facilitate, oversee*)
processes (*exemplify*)
profits (*maximize*)
programme (*comprehensive*)
programmes (*align, comprehensive, implement*)
progress (*monitor, signify*)
proportion (*substantial*)
purpose (*functional*)

question (*frame, hypothetical, refine*)
questions (*formulate, fundamental, guiding, preliminary*)

rate (*equivalent*)
reading (*extensive*)
reason (*plausible*)
reasons (*articulate, conflicting*)
recommendations (*endorse*)
records (*cumulative, disclose*)
recovery (*partial*)
relations (*intensify*)
relationship (*establish, infer*)
report (*verify*)

reports (*contradictory*)

requirements (modify)

research (*coordinate, extensive, situate*)

resources (*allocate*)

response (*robust*)

responses (*elicit, generate*)

results (*definitive, optimal*)

review (*comprehensive, extensive, systematic, undertake*)

reward (*intrinsic*)

risk (*constitute, cumulative, intensify, magnitude, minimal, underlying*)

role (*assign, clarify, conventional, integral, partial, prominent*)

rules (*adhere, establish*)

sample (*normative*)

scale (*arbitrary*)

scenario (*hypothetical*)

score (*assign, cumulative, equivalent*)

services (*allocate, coordinate*)

setting (*feasible*)

situation (*desirable, hypothetical*)

size (*modify*)

skills (*acquire, advanced, attain, demonstrate, discrete, enhance, equip, functional, refine*)

society (*contemporary*)

solution (*desirable*)

solutions (*formulate*)

sources (*contemporary*)

spirit (*embody*)

stances (*exemplify*)

standards (*adhere*)

statement (*definitive*)

step (*conventional*)

strategies (*endorse, guiding, implement*)

strengths (*utilize*)

structure (*coherent*)

students (*prospective*)

study (*prospective*)

subjects (*exploration*)

success (*attain, attribute, replicate*)

system (*advanced, coherent, comprehensive, establish, oversee, robust, unified, utilize*)

targets (*attain*)

task (*accomplish, assign, discrete*)

teachers (*prospective*)

technique (*conventional*)

techniques (*advanced*)

technology (*advanced, implement, utilize*)

tensions (*manifest*)

text (*authentic*)

themes (*emerge, exemplify, exploration*)

theories (*formulate*)

theory (*unified*)

thinking (*clarify*)

thoughts (*articulate, clarify*)

threat (*renewed, substantial*)

time (*allocate, considerable*)

traditions (*adhere*)

training (*undertake*)

traits (*embody*)

treatment (*extensive, modify*)

understanding (*demonstrate, enhance, facilitate, gauge, refine*)

unit (*functional*)

units (*discrete*)

usage (*monitor*)

use (*extensive, functional, growing, intrinsic, monitor, preclude, systematic*)

value (*arbitrary, assign, comparable, inherent, intrinsic, normative, optimal*)

values (*discern, embody*)

variables (*omit*)

verdict (*definitive*)

victory (*decisive*)

view (*clarify, conventional, unified*)

views (*articulate, conflicting, gauge*)

violence (*prone*)

virtues (*inherent*)

way (*feasible*)

words (*omit*)

work (*situate*)

works (*contemporary*)

worth (*intrinsic*)

About the author

Steve Hart has been editing and proofreading for international academics and graduate students since 2005. He is the author of *English Exposed: Common Mistakes Made by Chinese Speakers*, has co-authored undergraduate English textbooks for the Indian market and written two practical grammar guides for university students. He is currently an academic coordinator and dissertation supervisor at a higher education institution in Cambridge, England.

Index: Top 200 by part of speech

The entries of the following index indicate the chapters in which the top 200 terms can be found, organized by part of speech.

Verbs

Adverbs

actively 1
arguably 2
collectively 4
inevitably 11
initially 12

notably 13
predominantly 15
primarily 16
relatively 17
reportedly 17

routinely 18
steadily 18
subsequently 19
sufficiently 19
undoubtedly 20

Adjectives

advanced 1
apparent 2
applicable 2
arbitrary 2
authentic 3
beneficial 3
characteristic 3
coherent 4
comparable 4
comprehensive 4
conflicting 4
considerable 5
constituent 5
contemporary 5
contradictory 5
conventional 6
cumulative 6
decisive 6
definitive 6
desirable 7
discrete 8

equivalent 9
explicit 9
extensive 10
feasible 10
functional 10
fundamental 10
growing 11
guiding 11
hypothetical 11
imperative 11
implicit 11
informed 12
inherent 12
instrumental 12
integral 12
intrinsic 13
marginal 13
minimal 13
normative 13
optimal 14
partial 14

persistent 15
pervasive 15
plausible 15
preliminary 15
prevalent 15
problematic 16
prominent 16
prone 16
prospective 16
renewed 17
respective 17
robust 18
salient 18
subjective 19
substantial 19
susceptible 19
systematic 19
theoretical 19
underlying 20
unified 20
viable 20

Nouns

adjustment 1
advent 1
ambiguity 2
amendment 2
apparatus 2
assumption 3
capability 3
complexity 4
conception 4
consistency 5
constraint 5
continuity 5
contributor 6

correlation 6
depiction 7
discourse 8
discrepancy 8
disparity 8
distinction 8
exploration 10
implication 11
insight 12
magnitude 13
notion 14
paradox 14
perception 14

premise 15
proponent 16
proximity 16
recognition 16
reliance 17
similarity 18
speculation 18
standing 18
suitability 19
tendency 19
trait 20
transition 20
variance 20

General index

This index has been deliberately designed so that only chapter numbers are given. Searching for the relevant entry within chapters will help to create links between the terms.

advent – top 200 term
adversary – general term
3 (attain) – see usage notes of entry in Ch. 3

1 – top 200 entry
1 – general reference
A – Appendix